Historical American Biographies

MATHEW BRADY

Photographer of the Civil War

Lynda Pflueger

Enslow Publishers, Inc.

40 Industrial Road   PO Box 38
Box 398   Aldershot
Berkeley Heights, NJ 07922   Hants GU12 6BP
USA   UK

http://www.enslow.com

To Sadie, for her squeaky serenades.

Copyright © 2001 by Lynda Pflueger

All rights reserved.

No part of this book may be reproduced by any means
without the written permission of the publisher.

Library of Congress Cataloging-in-Publication Data

Pflueger, Lynda.
  Mathew Brady : photographer of the Civil War / Lynda Pflueger.
    p. cm. — (Historical American biographies)
  Includes bibliographical references (p.) and index.
  ISBN 0-7660-1444-4
  1. Brady, Mathew B., 1823 (ca.)–1896—Juvenile literature. 2. Photographers—
United States—Biography—Juvenile literature. 3. Portrait photography—United
States—History—Juvenile literature. 4. United States—History—Civil War,
1861–1865—Photography—Juvenile literature. [1. Brady, Mathew B., 1823
(ca.)–1896. 2. Photographers. 3. Portrait photography—History. 4. United
States—History—Civil War, 1861–1865—Photography.] I. Title. II. Series.
  TR140.B68 P45 2001
  770'.92—dc21

                                                            00-010732

Printed in the United States of America

10 9 8 7 6 5 4 3 2

To Our Readers: We have done our best to make sure all Internet addresses in
this book were active and appropriate when we went to press. However, the
author and the publisher have no control over and assume no liability for the
material available on those Internet sites or on other Web sites they may link to.
Any comments or suggestions can be sent by e-mail to comments@enslow.com or
to the address on the back cover.

Illustration Credits: Enslow Publishers, Inc., pp. 59, 64; Library of
Congress, pp. 4, 10, 15, 17, 23, 24, 25, 26, 29, 30, 33, 37, 38, 40, 44,
52, 61, 69, 72, 73, 77, 86, 90, 92; Lynda Pflueger, p. 109; National
Archives, pp. 54, 57, 87, 88, 96, 99, 103, 106.

Cover Illustration: Library of Congress.

CONTENTS

Mathew Brady

1

WAR

In the spring of 1861, the United States was on the brink of a civil war. South Carolina, Mississippi, Alabama, Georgia, Florida, Louisiana, and Texas had seceded from the Union and formed the Confederate States of America. Confederate soldiers were taking over Union military facilities throughout the South. When Fort Sumter, in Charleston, South Carolina, fell into Confederate hands, President Abraham Lincoln called for seventy-five thousand volunteers to join the Union Army and bring the rebellious Southern states back into the Union.

Mathew Brady, the famous New York photographer, was determined to use his camera to record the historic events that were about to take place. He outfitted two wagons to act as traveling darkrooms.

Each wagon had a light-tight black canopy so that no light could get in and was equipped with shelves and compartments to hold chemicals, photographic plates, and other camera equipment. Brady approached President Abraham Lincoln for permission to go with the Union Army onto the battlefield. Lincoln wrote a pass for Brady, but told him that he had to finance the project himself.

"Forward to Richmond"

On Tuesday, July 16, 1861, thirty thousand Union soldiers, under the command of General Irvin McDowell, marched south out of Washington, D.C., into Virginia. As the soldiers left the city, bands played loudly and flags waved in the air. "Forward to Richmond" was their battle cry. Their goal was to capture Richmond, the capital of the Confederacy, and end the Southern rebellion.

Following closely behind the soldiers were hundreds of civilians. Congressmen, senators, and other influential men brought along their wives, daughters, and friends to see the big fight. They carried picnic baskets, champagne, camp chairs, and binoculars. They looked like they were going to a picnic instead of to a war. "We thought it wasn't a bad idea to have the great men from Washington come out to see us thrash the Rebs," one Union soldier commented.[1]

Sweating in the summer heat and covered with dust, Mathew Brady tried to keep up with McDowell's troops and make his way through the throng of civilians. He sat on the seat of one of his wagons wearing a long white linen jacket called a duster and a straw hat. Sitting beside him were Dick McCormick, a newspaperman, and Alfred Waud, a sketch artist for *Harper's Weekly* newspaper. Following closely behind in Brady's second wagon was Ned Hause, Brady's darkroom assistant.

The Confederates already knew that the Union Army was coming, thanks to Rose O'Neal Greenhow, a Confederate spy living in Washington, D.C. Greenhow had sent a coded message hidden in the hair of a young Southern sympathizer to General Pierre Beauregard, the commander of the Confederate forces. Beauregard immediately sent for reinforcements and stationed his men along an eight-mile section of a small stream called Bull Run, a few miles outside of Centreville, Virginia.

Battle of Bull Run

When the Union Army reached Centreville, on July 18, Union General McDowell was forced to delay his attack. His supply wagons had not kept up with the main body of his army. His men were in need of food and other supplies. While waiting, he sent a group of his men on a reconnaissance (scouting) mission to test the Confederates' strength in the area. Brady learned about the advance and received permission to accompany the soldiers.

After traveling a short distance, the Northern soldiers had a fierce confrontation with Confederate forces at Blackburn's Ford. After this battle, the Union soldiers retreated. During the battle, Brady was too close to the fighting. The sound of cannon and gunfire frightened his horses. Brady and his companions leaped out of their wagons, grabbed the reins, and threw their jackets over their horses' heads. This calmed the horses enough so that they could be led away from the battle. From this experience, Brady learned that, during a battle, he needed to keep his distance from the front line. Otherwise, he risked losing his costly photographic equipment.

Two days later, on Sunday, July 21, McDowell ordered his Union troops to attack. The inexperienced soldiers fought better than their commanders had expected. By early afternoon, it appeared that the Union would be victorious. Then, the tide of the battle changed. The Confederates, under the command of Thomas Jackson, refused to give way on Henry House Hill. His tenacity earned Jackson the nickname "Stonewall" Jackson.

The Confederates rallied and began a counterattack. In time, they broke through the Union lines and the Union soldiers began to withdraw. At first, the soldiers' retreat was orderly, but it turned into a panic as the Confederate soldiers chased them.

During the battle, Brady positioned himself on high ground near a house owned by the Matthew family a few miles from the battle. As he was returning to the main road, he was engulfed by the retreating Union soldiers and frightened civilians. Several carriages and wagons were overturned and blocked the road. Soldiers and civilians fought each other to make

Captured

New York Congressman Alfred Ely was one of the many civilian spectators who came out to see the Battle of Bull Run. Ely learned the hard way that witnessing a battle was not a form of entertainment. During the battle, he became impatient to find out what was going on. He ventured out onto the battlefield, where he was captured by a group of Confederate soldiers. They took him to Richmond as a prisoner of war. While confined, he kept a journal and wrote, "I found that to visit battle-fields as a mere pastime . . . is neither a safe thing in it self, nor a justifiable use of the passion which Americans are said to possess for public spectacle."[2]

their way through the crowd. Brady set up his camera and took photographs of the frightened mob.

When night fell, the Confederate shelling ceased, and it began to rain. Brady lost track of his friends. Exhausted, he led his horse into the woods and fell asleep on the wagon seat. Sometime during the night, a Union soldier from a New York regiment awakened Brady. He warned Brady that the woods were full of stragglers from both armies and tried to convince him to leave his wagon and join him on foot. Brady, however, was unwilling to leave his equipment. The soldier gave Brady a broadsword for protection. As he disappeared into the darkness, the soldier said he "wasn't going to stop retreating until he reached New York."[3]

Photo taken
July 22ⁿᵈ
1861

BRADY
The Photographer
returned from
Bull Run

Mathew Brady posed for this photograph shortly after he returned from the Battle of Bull Run on July 22, 1861. Note the outline of a broadsword under his jacket.

Brady was left alone for the rest of the night. Rain beat down on the top of his wagon. In the distance, he could hear the sounds of injured men on the battle-field. About dawn, he headed out again. When he finally reached the road, it was covered with things left behind by the fleeing soldiers and civilians the day before: shoes, coats, hats, broken wagons, haversacks, abandoned artillery, blood-soaked blankets, and dead horses. Occasionally, he ran into civilians looking for family members who had fallen in the battle.

Late that afternoon, Brady arrived in Washington, D.C. He immediately went to see his wife, Julia, and then went to his studio to develop his photographic plates. Before he left his studio, he stopped before a camera and had his picture taken. He was still wearing his straw hat. Underneath his duster, the outline of a broadsword could be seen.

News spread quickly that Brady had returned with photographs of the great battle, the first full-blown confrontation of the Civil War. *Humphrey's Journal* wrote, "Brady has shown more pluck than many of the officers and soldiers who were in the fight."[4] Later, when friends asked Brady why he took on such a dangerous project, he replied, "I felt I had to go. . . . a spirit in my feet said go, and I went."[5]

2

EARLY YEARS

Mathew Brady was born in 1823 in Warren County, New York. The exact date of his birth is unknown. His parents, Andrew and Julia Brady, were Irish immigrants. They came to the United States in 1820, settled in Upstate New York, and worked a small farm. No more is known about his family or childhood.

Evidently, Mathew suffered from an inflammation of the eyes that weakened his eyesight. When he was a teenager, he went to a health resort in Saratoga Springs, New York, in search of a cure. At the time, it was believed that treatment with natural spring waters could cure many diseases.

In Saratoga Springs, Mathew met William Page, a twenty-eight-year-old artist. Page painted historical scenes and portraits. He was impressed with Brady's artistic ability. Brady later said that Page "took an interest" in him and gave him "a bundle of his crayons [crayon drawings] to copy."[1] Brady studied the art of drawing portraits under Page's instruction.

New York City

In 1839, Page went to New York City and took Brady with him. New York City was a noisy, fast-paced, growing city. Hundreds of immigrants arrived each month from England, Scotland, Ireland, and Germany. Business was booming and this atmosphere provided many exciting opportunities for talented young men.

Page opened an art studio on Chambers Street. Shortly after arriving in the city, he introduced Brady to one of his former teachers, Samuel F. B. Morse, an inventor and professor of fine arts at the University of the City of New York. Brady later wrote that Morse was making a living "painting portraits at starvation prices."[2]

Morse had recently returned from Paris, France, where he had gone to patent the telegraph, his latest invention. The telegraph was a machine that sent coded messages over wires using electricity. While in Paris, Morse learned about the new science of photography. He met Louis Daguerre, a French scientist who had discovered how to fix an image permanently on a thin sheet of silver-plated copper. This image resulting from Daguerre's process was named daguerreotype.

History of Photography

The first camera was called a camera obscura, which means dark chamber. It consisted of a large box with a lens on one side and an eyepiece on the other. The inside of the box was completely dark. The only light that entered the box was through the lens. The objects on which the lens focused were reflected by mirrors onto a view screen at the bottom of the box. Artists used this crude camera as a sketching tool.

Since a camera obscura could only project, not record images, scientists in the eighteenth century looked for a way to make the reflected images permanent. In 1826, Joseph N. Niepce, a French inventor, coated a metal plate with a light-sensitive chemical, exposed it to light in a camera obscura for eight hours, and recorded the image on the plate. This became the world's first photograph.

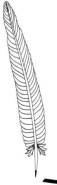

Louis Daguerre took Niepce's process a step further. In a camera obscura, he exposed an image on a sheet of silver-coated copper for five to ten minutes, removed the sheet from the camera, developed it in mercury vapor, and then fixed it (made it permanent) on the sheet with table salt. The resulting photograph was called a daguerreotype, in Daguerre's honor. The French government gave Daguerre a lifetime pension for making the process for creating a daguerreotype available to the public.

Morse was excited about the possibility of using this technique "to reduce the labor" needed to paint his portraits.[3] He planned to make daguerreotypes of his subjects and then make copies instead of having his customers pose for long periods of time.

Developing the telegraph had left Morse penniless. His salary from the university was not enough for him to live on, so he decided to supplement his income by giving lessons on the new daguerreotype process. Brady was one of his first students. Brady later recalled that, after meeting Morse, his life was "inextricably enmeshed with the infant art of photography."[4]

Brady of Broadway

In 1844, at the age of twenty-one, Brady opened his own photographic studio on the fourth floor of a building on the corner of Broadway and Fulton Street. At the time, Broadway was a long street filled with stores where everything was for sale—"all signs, all faces, all advertisements,

Samuel F. B. Morse instructed Brady in the new art of photography called "daguerreotype." This portrait of Morse hung in Brady's Washington gallery.

all voices, all outward aspects of things" urged a person to buy.[5]

Brady called his studio Brady's Daguerrian Miniature Gallery. On the first floor of the building, in the street-level windows, he hung examples of his work. Inside the entrance, a hand was painted on the wall with the forefinger pointing up the stairs. Underneath the hand was a sign that read "THREE FLIGHTS UP."

Brady worked hard at his new job. He spared no expense to make his studio as attractive and functional as possible. He hired the best staff, bought the finest equipment, and lavishly decorated his gallery. Because a photographer needed a great deal of natural light to take a good picture, Brady had skylights installed in the roof of his studio. Brady was one of the first photographers to use this technique.[6]

Brady's studio was open from 8:00 A.M. until 6:00 P.M. At first, his customers were mostly families. He often photographed children. Once customers climbed the three flights of steps to the studio, they were usually met by Brady himself, with his thick, steel-rimmed glasses and unruly dark hair. Brady greeted customers politely and guided them through the photographic process.

If the customers were not wearing clothes appropriate for picture taking, Brady would take them to a changing room, where they could put on dark-colored jackets or dresses. Light-colored clothes exposed faster than dark-colored clothes and stood out too much in the final photograph.

A daguerreotype of two unidentified sisters who were photographed in Mathew Brady's studio. Parents often brought their children to Brady's studio to be photographed.

Next, Brady would seat his customers in front of a camera. The large box-like camera was mounted on a tripod, or three-legged stand.

The lighting in the room was adjusted through the use of curtains, mirrors, and screens, so that no shadows would appear over the faces of his clients.[7] Brady often used a clamp called an immobilizer. It fastened around his customers' heads to help them sit up straight and stay still. The immobilizer could not be seen by the camera.

When posing his subjects, Brady looked for the camera angle that would flatter them most. He wanted his subjects to look as natural as possible and usually had them sit in a chair or stand while leaning on a prop. Brady also tried to make up for any physical defects his subjects might have. If his customer had a lot of freckles, Brady would rub the customer's face until it was bright red so that the skin would look evenly colored instead of blotchy. If a customer had sunken cheeks, Brady would place cotton in the cheeks to make them look fuller. Also, Brady often used wax to keep customers' ears from sticking out while they were being photographed.

When the customer was ready and the camera focused, a sheet of copper that had been prepared ahead of time was placed in the camera. The copper plate had been coated with silver, cleaned, and polished. Then it was exposed to iodine vapors at room temperature until its silver surface turned a golden yellow color. The aroma of the iodine vapor filled the whole gallery.

Daguerreotypes

Historian William Stapp wrote in *Facing the Light: Historic American Portrait Daguerreotypes* that daguerreotypes were more beautiful than any other photographic technique. Because the images were captured on a shiny mirror-like surface, they had an elusive quality. They flickered. A daguerreotype had to be held at just the right angle to see the image.

Daguerreotypes were one-of-a-kind images. No negative was produced during the process. They were also mirror images. The image on the plate was reversed from the way the image appeared in real life. Since daguerreotypes were considered a work of art, they were usually enclosed in a small case.

At this point, Brady would instruct his client not to move a muscle. The camera lens cover would be removed from the camera and the plate exposed for five to fifteen seconds. (Brady left no record of the exact exposure times he used.) Then the lens cap would be placed back on the camera and the subject could move again.

After the glass plate was developed by exposing it to mercury vapor at 167°F, the plate was rinsed in a bath of hyposulfite of soda and washed in distilled water. The picture was dried, mounted under glass to protect it, and enclosed in a case that the customer had selected. Brady charged three to five dollars for a daguerreotype. The back of each photograph was stamped "Photographed by Brady."[8] This was Brady's trademark.

In 1844, there were ninety-six photographic studios making daguerreotypes in New York City. Six of Brady's top competitors were also located on Broadway. Despite the competition, the New York press acknowledged Brady as the leader in the new field shortly after his studio opened.[9]

Friends and Supporters

Although Brady's studio was an immediate success, it is doubtful he financed the whole operation himself. No records exist, but it is likely that Brady's former employer and friend A. T. Stewart, a department store merchant, invested in Brady's gallery. Another possible financial backer may have been P. T. Barnum, who owned the American Museum down the street from Brady's gallery. In his museum of curiosities, Barnum displayed midgets, giants, fat ladies, skinny men, Siamese twins, and other unusual characters. In time, Barnum became known as the Great American Showman. He sent Brady customers every time he had a chance.[10]

Awards

In later years, Brady estimated that he had taken thousands of photographs during his first few years in the business.[11] He not only practiced and became more skilled at his art, but he discovered new ways to improve it. He discovered a method for making daguerreotypes in color.[12] The process involved coating ivory plaques with a mixture of chemicals that are sensitive to light. After being exposed and developed, the plaques were hand-tinted. When Brady's color daguerreotypes first appeared, they were an instant success. They became "the order and style of the day."[13]

When the American Institute of Photography held its first photographic competition in 1844, Brady entered the contest and won first honors. The following year, he entered again. This time, he received awards for the best colored and the best plain daguerreotypes. The awards were good for business and brought in more customers. In less than two years, Brady had become known as Brady of Broadway. His reputation for artistic excellence spread beyond the boundaries of the city.

3

GALLERY

In 1845, Brady began collecting images of important Americans. He thought that, if he photographed former presidents, statesmen, writers, great actors and actresses, visiting royalty, and high-ranking military officers, "his business would be self-perpetuating— one sitting advertising the next."[1] In addition, Brady felt he had a duty to act as a photographic historian. "From the first," he later said, "I regarded myself as under obligation to my country to preserve the faces of its historic men and women."[2]

The first subject for his historic gallery was Andrew Jackson, the seventh president of the United States. Jackson, who was nicknamed Old Hickory because of his toughness, was now an invalid confined to his bed at his home, the Hermitage, in Nashville,

Tennessee. Brady later said he sent a photographer to Jackson's home "barely in time to save" his likeness for future generations to see.[3]

Jackson's family and doctor did not want the photograph to be taken, but Jackson insisted that it be done. On the morning the photographer was to arrive, Jackson rose from his sick bed and paid special attention to the way he dressed. Then he sat in a chair propped up by pillows and cushions. When it was time for the photograph to be taken, Jackson "nerved himself up with the same energy that characterized his whole life, and his eye was stern and full of fire."[4] After the photograph was taken, Jackson returned to his bed. A few days later, he died.

Washington, D.C., Studio

Though the exact date is not known, sometime in 1849, Brady opened a small Daguerrian Gallery in Washington, D.C., at Four-and-a-half Street and Pennsylvania Avenue.

This daguerreotype of Andrew Jackson was "the most important one of Jackson's existence," according to Charles H. Hart, an art expert. Brady sent Dan Adams, a young photographer from Nashville, Tennessee, to Jackson's home to photograph him in 1845.

The gallery operated mainly when Congress was in session.

One day, Brady photographed the current president of the United States, Zachary Taylor, and his Cabinet. According to critic C. Edwards Lester, Brady was the "only daguerreotypist in America to be favored by a *visit at his studio* from the President and his cabinet."[5]

While in Washington, D.C., Brady photographed Dolley Madison, the widow of the fourth president of the United States, James Madison. During her husband's administration, famous author Washington Irving had written that Mrs. Madison was "a fine, portly, buxom dame, who has a smile and a pleasant word for everyone."[6] After her husband's death in 1836, Mrs. Madison moved back to Washington, D.C., where she was the queen of official Washington society and took part in all the city's social affairs. Mrs. Madison was eighty years old when Brady

Dolley Madison was one of the most popular First Ladies to grace the city of Washington, D.C.

photographed her in her home on Lafayette Square, near the White House.

On February 14, 1849, Brady went to the White House to photograph the eleventh president of the United States, James Polk. When Polk came out of his study to greet his guest, Brady asked what room in the executive mansion had the most natural light. Polk led the way to the dining room, where Brady set up his equipment. When everything was ready, Brady asked Polk to sit still and took the lens cover off his camera. He counted the number of seconds he felt it would take to capture Polk's image. Then he put the cover back on the lens, thanked President Polk, and left. Polk went back to his office and wrote in his diary, "I yielded to the request of an artist named Brady of New York by sitting for my daguerreotype likeness today. I sat in the large dining room."[7]

Another prominent American photographed in Brady's Washington studio was John C.

James Polk was president of the United States from 1845 to 1849. Mathew Brady took this photograph on February 14, 1849. Four months later, Polk died at his home in Nashville, Tennessee.

Mathew Brady photographed John C. Calhoun during the winter of 1849 and used this image to create many portraits, including a large painting that hung in his studio.

Calhoun of South Carolina. Calhoun had been the vice president of the United States from 1825 to 1832. He had run several times for the presidency but was never elected. He had also served in the United States House of Representatives and the Senate and had held the offices of secretary of war and secretary of state. Sometime in 1849, Calhoun came to Brady's studio to be photographed. Calhoun's daughter wanted a picture of her father for her locket. It was a cloudy, rainy day and Calhoun was concerned that the bad weather would prevent Brady from taking a good likeness of him. Brady assured Calhoun that taking a longer exposure of him would make up for poor lighting conditions. Calhoun had to pose three times before Brady was satisfied with the results. Brady later recalled that Calhoun's most outstanding feature was his eyes. Brady said that they were "startling, and almost hypnotized me."[8]

Juliet Handy

While working in Washington, D.C., Brady met and fell in love with Juliet Elizabeth Handy, the daughter of Samuel Handy, a well-known lawyer. Her family called her Julia. She had been born in Somerset County, Maryland. In his later years, Brady commented that their courtship "took place against the backdrop of a beautiful Maryland plantation—gay parties, hoopskirts, and young men who talked of nothing else but horses, duels and manners of the time."[9] Brady also said that the "happiest moment of his life was on that evening when he took Julia into his arms and glided across the [dance] floor to the strains of a beautiful waltz."[10]

Reverend George Samson married the couple in his Baptist church on E Street in Washington, D.C., sometime in 1849 or 1850. The exact date of the ceremony is unknown. After their wedding, they moved into the National Hotel in Washington, D.C.

Shortly after his marriage, Brady had a falling out with his landlord, a jeweler who owned the building that housed his Washington gallery. When his lease was up, he decided not to renew it. Brady returned to New York City with his wife. They moved into the Astor Hotel, one of New York City's most fashionable hotels. The hotel was conveniently located opposite his New York gallery. This gave Brady the chance to promote his business with the many celebrities who stayed at the Astor while visiting New York City.

New York City Studio

During the winter of 1849, Brady photographed Henry Clay in his New York studio. A leading statesman for almost fifty years, Clay had served as the speaker of the House of Representatives, a member of the United States Senate, and as secretary of state. He became known as the Great Compromiser because of his repeated efforts to settle the bitter disputes over slavery between the Northern and Southern states.

When Brady first approached Clay about photographing him, Clay refused. He said that he had no time to sit for a "counterfeit presentment."[11] Clay felt a photograph was a poor substitute for a real portrait.

Mathew Brady posed for this photograph with his wife, Julia Handy Brady (on left), and Mrs. Haggerty (on right), who may have been a relative. This photograph shows the qualities that were most admired in Brady's work—natural expressions on the sitters' faces and a harmonious setting.

Later, Brady discovered that several of Clay's friends wanted a likeness of him. They were able to persuade the Kentucky statesman to visit Brady's studio.

On the day Clay was to arrive, a crowd gathered to see the great statesman. But Clay had been held up at a party given in his honor at city hall. He sent word for Brady to join him there. When Brady arrived, he chose an empty room near where Clay's reception was being held and set up his equipment. Brady's assistants tacked curtains over the windows. As Clay entered the room, he announced, "Well, here I am Mr. Brady."[12]

Brady showed Clay to a chair in front of his camera and guided him into an appropriate pose with his hands in his lap. By the time Brady returned to his camera, a crowd of people from Clay's reception had filled the room. The well-wishers blocked Brady's view. He patiently waited for them to move out of the way. Finally, Clay raised one of his hands and called for silence. People moved out of the way of the

Henry Clay was a charming, generous, and eloquent speaker. He became one of the most idolized men of his time.

camera and froze. Clay resumed his pose and Brady was able to take his photograph. Brady was not happy with the sitting and made Clay promise that he would visit his studio before he left the city.

In the spring of 1849, Edgar Allan Poe, a famous poet, short-story writer, and literary critic came to Brady's studio. Poe had written the famous poem "The Raven." Poe accompanied a friend, William Ross Wallace, another poet, who had arranged for Brady to take his photograph. Brady also wanted to photograph Poe and asked him if he would be willing to sit for a portrait. Poe said no. Brady suspected that Poe refused because he did not have the money to pay for the portrait. Brady explained that he was a fan of Poe's work and wanted a photograph of him to hang in his gallery. Once again, Poe refused. When Brady said there would be no charge, Poe finally agreed. Poe died just a few months after Brady photographed him.

During the summer of 1849, Brady wanted to photograph Daniel Webster, the famous orator who spoke for a strong national government and once said, "Liberty *and* Union, now and for ever, one and inseparable!"[13] In order to achieve his goal, Brady recruited one of their mutual friends, Charles Stetson, Jr. Stetson promised Brady that he would do his best to talk Webster into sitting for a portrait. Instead of making an appointment, he would signal Brady that Webster was coming by waving a handkerchief from the window in the Astor Hotel where Webster was staying. All Brady could do was post a lookout and wait for the signal.

Two days later, Stetson kept his promise. The signal was seen in a hotel window. Shortly afterward, Stetson and Webster went to Brady's gallery. Webster's entrance was somewhat theatrical. When he entered the studio, he announced in a booming voice, "Mr. Brady, I am here, sir! I am clay in the hands of the potter! Do with me as you will, sir!"[14] Then he shook hands with Brady.

While photographing Webster, Brady noted that the statesman's large, deep-set eyes seemed to "hide mysteries in their depths" and that when his assistant tightened the immobilizer clamp around his head, Webster's thin lips seemed to compress tighter with each turn of the thumbscrew.[15] Three photographs were taken that day. When the session was over, instead of saying good-bye, Webster simply bowed and left the gallery.

Gallery of Illustrious Americans

With his exhibit of "Illustrious Americans" now complete on his gallery wall, Brady decided to publish a book of his portraits. He hired Francis D'Avignon, a noted French artist, to make lithographic copies of his daguerreotypes. (A lithograph is a print made from a flat, prepared stone or plate.) Brady paid D'Avignon one hundred dollars for each print. He also hired C. Edwards Lester to write a biographical sketch of each person included in the book. At first, Brady intended to include twenty-four famous Americans, but he changed his mind. When the book was published, only twelve illustrious Americans were included: Daniel

Daniel Webster was a well-known American orator famous for his memorable words, "Liberty and Union, now and forever, one and inseparable!"

Webster, Henry Clay, John Calhoun, Zachary Taylor, former President Millard Fillmore, explorer John C. Frémont, General Winfield Scott, statesman Lewis Cass, politician Silas Wright, historian William H. Prescott, naturalist John J. Audubon, and clergyman William E. Channing.

On January 1, 1850, the book, entitled *Gallery of Illustrious Americans*, was published. The volume was bound in a handsome leather cover with the title printed in gold. It weighed five pounds and sold for thirty dollars, a high price for the times. The book received excellent reviews from New York newspapers but did not sell well. Brady eventually cut the price of the book in half in an effort to sell more copies. Although the book did not make a lot of money, it increased business in Brady's studio. People wanted to have their photographs taken in the same studio where so many famous Americans had been photographed.

FAME

In 1850, Queen Victoria of England announced that her country would hold a great industrial exhibition, the first World's Fair, in the spring of the following year. A huge structure called the Crystal Palace was being built in Hyde Park, London, to house the exhibition. The building would cover more than twenty-one acres and be built entirely of glass in an iron framework. Prizes would be awarded at the exhibition and photography was one of the major categories for competition.

Photographers from all over the world, especially New York, began to prepare for the big event. Competition was fierce. Several photographers tried to come up with interesting subjects for their entries. One looked for "any man or woman over one hundred years old" to photograph.[1] Another advertised in a trade journal for "a Revolutionary veteran to come forward to have his likeness taken FREE."[2] Another looked for "twins or triplets, all over eighty" to photograph.[3]

Brady did not advertise for odd or unusual subjects. In his files he had a large number of photographs of prominent Americans, both living and dead. He gathered a collection of forty-eight photographs and prepared to have them shipped to the exhibition's Photographic Committee in London.

Europe

Brady and his wife, Julia, sailed to Europe aboard the S.S. *Arago* on July 12, 1851. They planned to attend the Great Industrial Exposition and then travel through Europe for a year. According to an article in the *Daguerrean Journal*, Brady hoped to visit Louis Daguerre, the "father of the new art" of daguerreotype while in Europe.[4] Unfortunately, Daguerre died at his home in France the same day Brady sailed from New York.

The trip to Europe was meant to give Brady a chance to display his work overseas. Also, it was time for Brady to take a greatly needed rest. He had worked constantly, building his career, for the last seven years. His health had suffered. His eyes were weaker and his eyesight had grown so bad that he rarely used a camera himself anymore. Earlier in the year, the *Photographic Art Journal* reported that Brady was not taking photographs himself due to his "failing eyesight," which prevented "the possibility of his using the camera with any certainty. But he is an excellent artist, nevertheless, understands his business perfectly and gathers about him the finest talent to be found."[5]

The photographic exhibition was the largest ever seen. Photographers from six countries (England, France, Italy, Germany, Austria, and the United States) exhibited seven hundred photographs. When the awards were announced, three out of the five medals were awarded to Americans. John D. Whipple from Boston won a medal for his one-by-one-inch picture of the moon taken through the telescope at Harvard.[6] His photograph was one of the first examples of astronomical photography. Martin M. Lawrence, one of Brady's competitors from New York, received a medal for his daguerreotype of three young women, each facing a different direction. Lawrence called his image "Past, Present, and Future." Brady received his medal for the "collective excellence" of his work.[7]

The exhibition's official report on the competition stated:

> On examining the daguerreotypes contributed by the United States, every observer is struck by their beauty of execution, the broad and well tinted masses of light and shade, and the total absence of all glare, which render them so superior to many works in the class.[8]

Horace Greeley, the editor of the *New York Tribune*, later wrote to Mathew Brady, "In picture-taking we beat the world."[9]

Second New York Gallery

In July 1852, the accounting firm of R. G. Dunn & Company stated in Brady's financial report that Brady

THE PRIZE MEDAL

Was awarded, at the Great Exhibition of the Industry of All Nations, in London, 1851,

TO M. B. BRADY,

FOR THE BEST DAGUERREOTYPES.

Mathew Brady won this prize medal for submitting the best overall daguerreotypes at the Great Industrial Exposition in London, England.

had established a highly successful business and that he owned real estate, railroads, bonds, and stock. The report also noted that Brady "likes to live a pretty fast life and spends his money freely," but added that he "deals honorably . . . is worthy of all confidence, and can buy all he wants freely."[10]

With his financial success and the awards he had received in Europe, Brady decided to open a second photographic studio in New York City. *Humphrey's Journal*, one of the leading photography publications at the time, wrote: "Mr. B's [Brady's nickname] Rooms are situated at 359 Broadway, in the most

Horace Greeley, founder of the New York Tribune *newspaper, served on the panel of judges at the Great Industrial Exhibition in London, England.*

central part of the city."[11] Brady chose the two floors of the building located above Thompson's Dining Saloon, a location frequented by many New Yorkers.

Brady designed the gallery himself. He ordered a huge double-faced skylight that was shaped like a pointed roof for the top floor and lavishly decorated the gallery. It opened in March 1853. *Humphrey's Journal* covered the gala opening and described the new gallery in detail:

> This room is twenty-six by forty feet, and is the largest Reception Room in this city. . . . The floors are carpeted with superior velvet tapestry. . . . The walls are covered with satin and gold paper. . . . Suspended on the walls, we find the Daguerreotypes of Presidents, Generals, Kings, Queens, Noblemen. . . . Adjoining the Reception Room is the business office of the establishment [that contains] a variety of showcases, where can be seen samples of all the various styles of Frames, Cases, Lockets . . . used in the Art.[12]

Wet-plate Process

At the time Brady opened his second New York gallery, a new photographic technique was about to revolutionize the field of photography. The new technique was called the wet-plate process. This new process made daguerreotypes obsolete. It allowed a photographer to produce a negative from which countless prints could be made. The photographer could also use these negatives to make enlargements of his images.

This drawing of the reception room in Brady's gallery appeared in Frank Leslie's Illustrated Newspaper.

The wet-plate process was developed by Frederick Scott Archer, an English sculptor and photographer. Archer coated a glass plate with a mixture of silver salts and collodian—a moist, sticky substance made by dissolving cotton treated with nitrate and sulfuric acids in a mixture of alcohol and ether. Once the wet-plate was exposed to light in a camera for a few seconds, it could be developed into a negative. This procedure was called the wet-plate process because the glass plate had to be exposed to light and developed before the mixture dried.

Alexander Gardner

In 1856, Brady had the good fortune to hire Alexander Gardner, a photographer who had immigrated to the United States from Scotland. Gardner had experience with the wet-plate process. He was a few years older than Brady and had been schooled in the sciences, particularly astronomy, botany, and chemistry. Before coming to the United States, he had worked as a jeweler, manager of a discount loan company, newspaper editor, and photographer.

Gardner and Brady worked well together. In a short time, Gardner began managing the studio and talked Brady into hiring a bookkeeper. This gave Brady more time to promote his business. At first, Brady did not like the formality of standard business procedures, but he soon realized how profitable his business could be if it were run well.

Gardner also had experience in making large, life-sized prints called imperials. With a wet-plate negative, images could be enlarged to seventeen by twenty-one inches and touched up to look like paintings. Brady loved the large imperials. He charged anywhere from fifty to seven hundred fifty dollars for them when they were finished in oil paints or crayons.[13] One of Brady's competitors claimed that there was "nothing Imperial about them except their price."[14]

National Photographic Art Gallery

At the age of thirty-four, with his business prospering, Brady decided to give Washington, D.C., another try. He opened a gallery at 350–352 Pennsylvania Avenue

Rogues' Gallery

In 1859, New York photographers joined with the police to fight crime by establishing the first official Rogues' Gallery. (A rogue is a tricky or dishonest person who leads a life of crime.) In a small room in the police headquarters building at Grand and Crosby streets hung four hundred fifty daguerreotypes of known criminals. When arrested, the criminals were forced to pose for the daguerreotypes. Then the portraits were classified by their crimes—pickpocket, con artist, burglar, etc.[15]

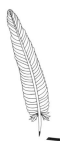

in January 1858. The gallery occupied the top three stories of a building that also housed a bank and a drugstore. Located on Washington's photography row, Brady called his new gallery the National Photographic Art Gallery. Brady brought Alexander Gardner to Washington, D.C., to manage the gallery. James Gardner, Alexander's brother, assisted him. Timothy O'Sullivan, one of Brady's photographers from New York City, also joined them.

In an advertisement in the *National Intelligencer*, Brady wrote that he "respectfully announces that he has established a Gallery of Photographic Art in Washington" and that he "is prepared to execute commissions for the Imperial Photograph, hitherto made only at his well-known establishment in New York."

Brady also pointed out that he brought to his Washington gallery "the results of fourteen years' experience in Europe and America."[16]

When Congress was in session, Brady and his wife spent a great deal of time in Washington, D.C. They became active in Washington society. Brady was listed as a member of the Washington Art Association and elected into membership of the American Society of Arts. In the spring of 1858, Brady and his wife attended a costume ball given by Senator William Gwin of California. Brady came to the ball dressed as Van Dyck, the famous painter.

In 1859, Brady opened a third gallery in New York City at 643 Bleecker Street. In 1860, he opened a fourth gallery at the intersection of Broadway and Tenth Street. He called this gallery the National Portrait Gallery.

Abraham Lincoln

Shortly after the opening of Brady's new gallery in New York City, Abraham Lincoln came to have his photograph taken. Lincoln, a lawyer from Illinois, was campaigning to be the Republican candidate for the presidency. Three members of the Young Men's Republican Committee accompanied Lincoln to Brady's gallery on February 27, 1860. That night, Lincoln was scheduled to give a speech at the Cooper Union. Founded by Peter Cooper, an inventor, manufacturer, and philanthropist, Cooper Union provided free adult education programs.

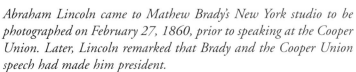

Abraham Lincoln came to Mathew Brady's New York studio to be photographed on February 27, 1860, prior to speaking at the Cooper Union. Later, Lincoln remarked that Brady and the Cooper Union speech had made him president.

Brady later recalled, "I had great trouble" posing Lincoln "when I got him before the camera."[17] Brady wanted to take a "natural picture," but Lincoln's appearance presented several problems.[18] He stood six feet four inches in height, his legs were long and out of proportion to his body, his ears stood out from his head, and his throat had a large Adam's apple. Finally, Brady decided to have Lincoln stand and place his hand on a book on a nearby table.

Brady was still not happy with the pose. He asked if he could rearrange Lincoln's collar.

"Ah," said Lincoln, "I see you want to shorten my neck."

"That's just it," Brady replied.[19] They both laughed, and the conversation seemed to relax Lincoln.

After his appearance at Cooper Union, Lincoln's speech was printed in the newspapers and pictures of him were in great demand. Lithographs made from Brady's photographs of Lincoln were published in *Frank Leslie's Illustrated* and *Harper's Weekly*. A touched-up version of the *Harper's* lithograph was widely circulated on campaign banners.

Cartes de visite

Around this time Brady's studios became involved in the latest craze in photography, a French novelty called *cartes de visite*, or visitor calling cards. The cards took the form of a two-and-one-fourth by three-and-one-half-inch photograph mounted on a two-and-one-half by four-inch card. Sometimes the person's name was written or printed on the bottom of the card. These cards could be mass-produced cheaply and were in great demand. Customers wanted cards of themselves, their family members, and of famous people. Collecting the cards and exchanging them became a popular activity. Soon manufacturers were making albums where the photographs could be easily mounted and stored.

Brady was not fond of the small cards. They were sold for ten to twenty-five cents apiece. He felt that they cheapened the art of photography.[20] Alexander Gardner, on the other hand, saw that they could make money producing the *cartes de visite*. He ordered special four-lens cameras that could take four to eight exposures at one time. He also established a contract with a photographic supply company, E. & H. T. Anthony & Co. of New York, to produce *cartes de visite* from images taken in Brady's studios. According to financial records, Brady's Washington studio earned four thousand dollars a year from this arrangement.

Prince of Wales

In the fall of 1860, nineteen-year-old Edward Albert, the Prince of Wales, arrived in the United States after touring Canada. This was the first time a member of the British royal family had visited the United States. He arrived in Detroit, Michigan, and then traveled to Washington, D.C., where he spent three days as the guest of President James Buchanan. Then he traveled to New York City where crowds followed him everywhere.

New York City firemen staged an evening torchlight procession in the prince's honor. The prince watched from the balcony of his Fifth Avenue hotel, while the firemen entertained him with blaring bands, acrobatics, and demonstrations of fire fighting. The Academy of Music also gave a dazzling Diamond Ball in his honor. Everyone who was socially prominent in New York City attended the affair. The prince enjoyed himself so much at the ball that he stayed until five o'clock in the morning.

All the photographers in New York City wanted to photograph the prince. Brady, however, was the one chosen by the prince himself. On the morning of October 13, a message was sent summoning Brady to the prince's hotel. The prince wanted to be photographed at Brady's studio but asked Brady to close his gallery to the public during his visit. Brady agreed, and returned to his studio to prepare for the prince's visit.

Shortly before noon, the prince and his party arrived. They toured the gallery, and then three imperial photographs were taken of the prince's entire party, followed by an imperial photograph of the prince alone. Afterward, photographs were taken of each member of the prince's party, individually and in small groups.

Curious as to why he had been chosen to photograph the prince, Brady asked the Duke of Newcastle, "Your Grace, might I ask to what I owe your favor to my studio?"

The duke replied, "Are you not the Mr. Brady, who earned the prize nine years ago in London? You owe it to yourself. We had your place of business down in our notebooks before we started."[21]

Success

Brady was now at the height of his career. He had become one of the most successful photographers in the world. He no longer had to seek out the rich and famous and persuade them to let him photograph them. They now sought him out.

5

A HOUSE
DIVIDED

In the fall of 1860, the United States was on the verge of civil war. Political differences between the North and the South and the controversy over slavery and states' rights were tearing the nation apart. Slavery had died a natural death in the North because of industrialization and the cheap labor provided by European immigrants. In the South, however, slavery flourished with the invention of the cotton gin. Developed by Eli Whitney, a Northern teacher, the gin separated the cotton fibers from the cottonseed a hundred times faster than a slave could by hand. This led to the growth of the textile industry. The demand for cotton soared until the Southern economy became dependent on slaves to produce it. Over the years, the North grew concerned that the South was trying to expand slavery to win political power. The South, on the other hand, worried that Northerners were trying to abolish slavery, and with it, their way of life.

The last straw for the South in the conflict was the election of Abraham Lincoln to the presidency. Many Southerners feared that Lincoln would do away with slavery and force them to free their slaves. According to the *Whig*, a newspaper in Richmond, Virginia, the election of Lincoln was "undoubtedly the greatest evil that has ever befallen this country" and the only thing left to do was to "prepare for a hurricane."[1]

When Abraham Lincoln was elected president, there were thirty-three states in the Union. By the time he arrived in Washington, D.C., for his inauguration, only twenty-six states remained.

Shortly after he arrived, Lincoln went to Brady's Washington studio to have his official inaugural portrait

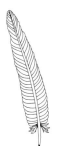

Washington Gallery

In 1860, a visitor to Brady's Washington gallery looked around the room at the portraits of prominent Americans hanging on the walls. There were Northerners, Southerners, Democrats, and Republicans. Some of them supported a state's right to secede from the Union and others called for a strong national government. "If only all the men pictured in this room could come together," the visitor commented, "how much more peaceful the nation would be."[2]

made. George Story, a portrait painter whose studio was in the same building as Brady's, watched the sitting. Later, he commented that Lincoln did not say a word and "seemed absolutely indifferent to all that was going on about him; —and he gave the impression that he was a man overwhelmed with anxiety and fatigue and care."[3]

Lincoln was accompanied to Brady's studio by Ward Lamon, a close friend and the city marshal of Washington, D.C. When Lincoln's sitting was over, Lamon realized that he had "not introduced Mr. Brady."[4] Lamon did not know that Brady had photographed Lincoln earlier. As Lincoln reached out his hand to Brady, he said, "Brady and the Cooper Union speech made me president!"[5]

Inauguration

A little past noon on March 4, 1861, President James Buchanan arrived at Willard Hotel to escort Lincoln to his swearing-in ceremony. Washington was a tense, quiet city that day. There were rumors of a Southern plot to take over Washington, D.C., and prevent the inauguration. Because of the rumors, infantrymen lined the parade route as the carriage carrying President James Buchanan and President-elect Lincoln rode down Pennsylvania Avenue. Army sharpshooters hid on the rooftops above the street.

At the unfinished Capitol Building, where the new president was to be sworn in, a battalion of District of Columbia troops lined the steps. Riflemen were placed in the windows of each wing of the building.

Plainclothes detectives mingled among the crowd of nearly ten thousand people that had gathered for the ceremony.

Brady and his crew set up their photographic equipment on the lawn of the Capitol. This was the first time an American president had been photographed during his swearing-in ceremony. Because of the tight security around Lincoln, Brady and his crew were unable to convince officials to let them move closer to the platform.

In his inaugural speech, Lincoln pleaded for peace. He declared that, although he hated the institution, he would not interfere with slavery where it had already

This daguerreotype shows Washington, D.C., prior to the Civil War. In the background is the unfinished Capitol.

been established. He would, however, keep it out of new territories. In conclusion, he declared to the South, "In *your* hands, my dissatisfied fellow country-men, and not in *mine*, is the momentous issue of civil war. . . . We are not enemies, but friends. We must not be enemies. Though passion may have strained, it must not break our bonds of affection."[6]

Everyone waited nervously for the swearing-in ceremonies to end and sighed with relief when no vio-lence took place. The mood had been so intense that one observer, Thomas Nast, a political cartoonist cov-ering the event for the *New York Illustrated News*, felt that a shout from the crowd or a single shot in the distance would have "inflamed the mob."[7]

Civil War

Six weeks after Lincoln's inauguration, Fort Sumter, a Union fort in Charleston, South Carolina, was seized by the Confederates. Lincoln immediately called for seventy-five thousand volunteers to join the Union Army and end the rebellion in the South. The states of Virginia, North Carolina, Arkansas, and Tennessee were not willing to fight against their Southern neighbors. They joined the Confederacy. The conflict between the Northern and the Southern states had finally erupted into civil war.

Almost overnight, Washington, D.C., turned into a military base. Every government building, including the basement of the unfinished Capitol, housed sol-diers. Brady's studio was filled with soldiers who wanted their photographs taken before they marched

This regiment of Union soldiers is dressed in uniforms typical of the French infantry. The men are wearing red caps, blue jackets, and baggy red trousers. Note the skylights on the right of the photograph.

off to war. They came alone, with their friends, or as entire regiments.

Lincoln appointed General Irvin McDowell commander of the Union forces. A West Point graduate, McDowell had never commanded a large force of men or fought in a big battle.[8] He felt he needed time to train his new volunteers. "This is not an army," he told Lincoln. "It will take a long time to make an army."

Lincoln replied, "You are green [inexperienced], it is true." He added, "but they [the Confederate soldiers] are green, also; you are all green alike."[9] Then he ordered McDowell to advance on the South.

On Sunday, July 21, the two armies met in the Battle of Bull Run. At first, it appeared that the Union Army would be victorious. Then the Confederates stood their ground and mounted a counterattack. In time, they broke through the Union lines and the Union soldiers began to withdraw.

The South won an important victory at the Battle of Bull Run. The North suffered an embarrassing defeat. The opportunity to win the war with one battle was lost forever. Both sides realized it would be a long fight.

6

FORWARD TO RICHMOND

After the Battle of Bull Run, Brady was determined to continue photographing the war, no matter what the cost. Julia, his wife, felt that his galleries in New York and Washington, D.C., were more important. She worried about the risks he would be taking on the battlefield. Brady later said, "My wife and my most intimate friends . . . looked unfavorably upon this departure from commercial business to pictorial war correspondence."[1]

Brady began to recruit photographers to work as teams. He wanted to have his men "in all parts of the army . . . like a rich newspaper" would do to cover the war.[2] He bought supplies and equipment for his photographers. Then he set up supply bases in strategic locations near the Union armies in the field. The cost of setting up his operations was huge, but Brady expected the sale of his "War Views" to repay his investment.[3]

Peninsular Campaign

Not happy with the job Irvin McDowell was doing, President Lincoln replaced him with General George B. McClellan. Thirty-four years old, McClellan had graduated second in his class at West Point. He served in the Mexican War and was a brilliant organizer and trainer. When McClellan took command of the Union Army of the Potomac, he established discipline among the troops. For six months, he drilled his men in the basics of soldiering.

Photographers on the battlefield with their " What-is-it wagon."

After constant urging by Lincoln and other public officials, McClellan finally came up with a plan to end the war. Once again, Richmond, the capital of the Confederacy, was the focus. Instead of taking his army over land, however, McClellan planned to float his forces down the Potomac River to Fort Monroe. The fort was located between the York and James rivers on the tip of the Virginia peninsula. From there, McClellan would march his army up the peninsula to Richmond. Lincoln, concerned about the safety of Washington, D.C., had doubts about the plan. After McClellan agreed to leave forty thousand soldiers behind to protect the capital, Lincoln allowed him to proceed.

Brady and McClellan were friends. Both were members of Tammany Hall, the Democratic political machine that ran New York City. When Brady asked to go along with the Union Army on the Peninsular Campaign, McClellan readily granted his request. From his Washington gallery, Brady recruited J. B. Gibson, D. G. Woodbury, and John Wood to go with him. Gibson and Wood would work as a team, and Woodbury would help Brady in the field.

In an amphibious (sea to land) operation that "had scarcely any parallel in history," McClellan's army traveled down the Potomac River to Fort Monroe.[4] It took three weeks and four hundred ships of various sizes and shapes to ferry 121,500 men, 14,952 horses and mules, 1,150 wagons, 44 artillery batteries, 74 ambulances, and supplies for all the men and livestock.[5] Brady's specially equipped darkroom wagons were transported with McClellan's baggage wagons.

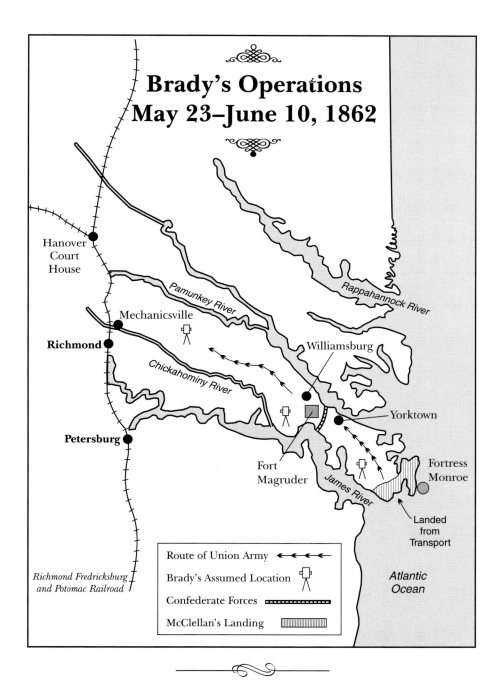

Brady's Operations May 23–June 10, 1862

Hanover Court House

Mechanicsville

Richmond

Pamunkey River

Rappahannock River

Williamsburg

Chickahominy River

Yorktown

Petersburg

Fort Magruder

James River

Fortress Monroe

Landed from Transport

Route of Union Army
Brady's Assumed Location
Confederate Forces
McClellan's Landing

Richmond Fredricksburg and Potomac Railroad

Atlantic Ocean

Mathew Brady followed the movements of the Union Army as it marched from May 23 through June 10, 1862.

When the photographers arrived at Fort Monroe, they began photographing scenes around the camp. Almost everyone, from the officers on McClellan's staff to the lowest-ranking soldier, was willing to pose for Brady's cameras. Many soldiers were curious about Brady's odd-looking wagons. They often asked, "What is it?" In time, the wagons became known as "what-is-it" wagons.

At dawn on April 4, McClellan's troops left Fort Monroe and advanced toward Yorktown, Virginia. Brady and his men joined a column of supply wagons. In a short time, it began to rain and the roads turned to mud. The column was forced to stop when it came to a bridge set on fire by the Confederates. It grew dark before the fire was put out, so the column camped for the night. Miserable in wet clothes, Brady and his men tried to sleep on the hard wagon seats. At dawn, they again fell in line with the supply wagons.

The following afternoon, the column approached Yorktown. The Confederates had settled themselves in extensive fortifications. McClellan thought the Confederate forces were larger than they actually were. Rather than attack, he ordered his men to bombard the Confederates with artillery.

While the men were getting ready for the assault, McClellan sent Professor Thaddeus Lowe into the sky in one of his hot-air balloons to spy on the Confederates. Lowe often stayed in the air all day at a height from which he could safely watch Confederate activity through his telescope. He made sketches and

Professor Thaddeus Lowe ascends into the sky in his hot-air balloon, the Intrepid, *during the Peninsular Campaign.*

used a telegraph to keep McClellan informed of Confederate movements.

After a month, nearly one hundred Union guns were in place and ready to fire on Yorktown. Before the bombardment could begin, however, the Confederates withdrew. McClellan immediately ordered his army forward to Richmond. Ten days later, they were forming a fifteen-mile front around the northeast side of the city.

Battle of Fair Oaks

On the night of May 30, a fierce rainstorm hit. Trees were uprooted and roads turned into rivers. The Chickahominy River overflowed its banks. The Union

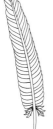

Up, Up, and Away!

Union Major General Fritz John Porter was fascinated with hot-air balloons. He accompanied Professor Thaddeus Lowe several times in his aerial observations and even learned how to operate a balloon. One day, Porter decided to go up by himself. As he rose into the sky, the balloon cable broke and the runaway balloon moved away "with incredible swiftness."[6] In a short time, Porter floated over the Confederate Army line and sharpshooters were preparing to fire on him. Mercifully, the wind shifted and pulled Porter back over to Union lines before the Confederates could shoot him down. When Porter finally got the balloon under control, it made a dramatic descent and struck a Union tent with great force when it landed. As Porter emerged unhurt from under the numerous folds of the balloon, he was greeted by cheering soldiers and a military band. McClellan, aware of General Porter's adventure, wrote his wife, "You may rest assured of one thing—you won't catch me in the confounded balloon. . . ."[7]

Army on the south side of the river was cut off from its supply line and reinforcements on the north side.

Taking advantage of the storm, Confederate General Joseph Johnston took the offensive. On the following morning, Johnston ordered his troops to attack McClellan's army in an area called Seven Pines near Fair Oaks, a small railroad station.

During the battle, Brady and Woodbury went to Professor Thaddeus Lowe's balloon camp outside Mechanicsville. Lowe was attempting to get his hot-air balloon, *Constitution*, into the air. The photographers set up their camera and photographed the scene. Several times during the day, Lowe rose into the air above the battle and then came down to telegraph his findings to General McClellan's headquarters. He told McClellan where it would be safe for his stranded soldiers to cross the Chickahominy River.

The Confederate advance pushed the Union soldiers back through the swampy terrain at Seven Pines. In some places, the water was knee to hip deep. As the Union soldiers were wounded, their comrades propped them up against tree stumps to keep them from drowning before they could receive medical care. The battle ended when General Johnston was severely wounded and the Confederate troops withdrew, falling back toward Richmond.

Brady and Woodbury photographed the battlefield. The swampy ground was covered with hundreds of dead soldiers and horses, rotting away. The stench was so bad that it overpowered the odor of the

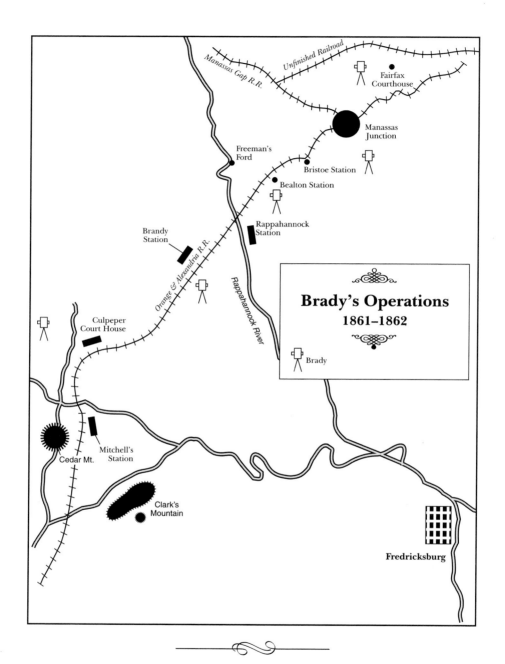

Mathew Brady and his staff covered the Civil War through several battles during 1861 and 1862.

chemicals the photographers used to develop their photographic plates.

Battle of Seven Days

After the Battle of Fair Oaks, both armies regrouped. General Robert E. Lee, took command of the Confederate Army. Lee, a West Point graduate, was a veteran of the Mexican War. He had also served as the commandant of the United States Military Academy at West Point. Shortly after taking command, Lee sent his former student, James Ewell Brown "J.E.B." Stuart, on a daring three-day ride around McClellan's army. From the information Stuart gave him, Lee decided to cross the Chickahominy River and attack the unprotected right flank of the Union Army. He hoped this would make McClellan withdraw from Richmond and force him to move his army south in order to secure his supply lines.

Lee ordered General Stonewall Jackson's troops down from the Shenandoah Valley and divided his

General Robert E. Lee
When the Civil War began, President Lincoln offered Robert E. Lee the command of the Union Army. Lee declined and remained loyal to his home state of Virginia. When Virginia seceded from the Union, Lee offered his services to the Confederacy. He eventually rose to become commander of all the Confederate troops.

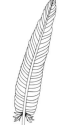

army, leaving only two Confederate divisions to guard Richmond. Then, on June 26, Lee attacked the unprotected right flank of the Union Army near Mechanicsville.

Once again, McClellan mistakenly believed that he was greatly outnumbered. He thought that Lee would not have divided his army if he did not have a superior force. After a fierce battle, McClellan ordered his troops to retreat six miles down the Chickahominy River to Gaines Mills. From there, McClellan planned to move his supply base south to Harrison's Landing. Then he would wait until he received reinforcements from Washington before trying again to capture Richmond.

Lee followed the Union troops as they withdrew southward. Since the Battle of Fair Oaks, Brady and Woodbury had been camped at Savage Station, a small railroad depot where a hospital had been established. On June 29, they were caught in the massive retreat. As they left Savage Station, Confederate shells began to hit the ground around them. They joined a column of supply wagons and were forced to leave the road to avoid troop movements.

During the night, they moved through the forest by torchlight. When it started to rain, the column stopped. Down the line, it was whispered that they were lost. A few minutes later, the column began to move again. Then the sounds of muffled wheels were heard nearby. The alarm was sounded. They feared that the Confederates were getting ready to fire on them. Just in time, one of the officers with the column recognized a familiar voice and called out. The sounds they heard had came from Union troops. The column regrouped and moved on toward White Oak Swamp.

Around midnight, Brady and Woodbury came across an abandoned barn. Exhausted, they parked their wagons and slept. Before long, they were awakened by a Union horseman who ordered them to rejoin the supply wagons. By daybreak, the Confederates had caught up with the Union column. The white covers on the supply wagons made perfect targets for the Confederate artillery. A shell struck the wagon in front of Brady's. The explosion frightened Brady's horses. They reared and almost overturned his wagon.

Finally, on July 1, the column reached Malvern Hill, where the Union Army made its final stand against Lee's relentless pursuit. During the battle, the supply column was moved to the rear and ordered off the road to make way for artillery and ambulances. Brady and Woodbury spent another sleepless night on their wagon boxes with nothing to eat but hardtack— a dry biscuit. When the battle ended, the supply column made its way to Harrison's Landing.

After seven days of fighting, both armies had paid a terrible price. The Confederates lost sixteen thousand men, and the Union Army lost twenty thousand. It had been a terrifying ordeal for Brady and his photographers. After photographing scenes at Harrison's Landing, Brady returned to Washington, D.C.

Brady mounted many of his photographs of the Peninsular Campaign on stereo cards and labeled them with titles. Stereo cards contain dual photographs of the same image. When the cards are seen through a viewer, called a stereoscope, the two images combine and appear as one three-dimensional image. Brady sold the stereo cards for seventy-five cents to a dollar each in his galleries.

The Second Battle of Bull Run

As McClellan made his way down the Virginia peninsula to Harrison's Landing, a new Union Army was forming—the Army of Virginia. The new army, commanded by Major General John Pope, consisted of units that had operated separately around Washington, D.C., and in the Shenandoah Valley. Instead of receiving reinforcements at Harrison's Landing, McClellan was ordered by Lincoln to join Pope in northern Virginia by way of the Chesapeake and Potomac rivers.

Lee realized that this new operation would give the Union Army "a powerful advantage." He had to act quickly.[8] After the last of the Seven Days battles, he sent his army north to meet the new threat. He ordered Stonewall Jackson's troops to cut off Pope's railroad supply line to Washington, D.C., and to loot the Union supply depot at Manassas Junction. On August 29, 1862, Pope's soldiers clashed with Jackson's troops near the site of the First Battle of Bull Run. When Jackson's men ran out of ammunition, they threw rocks at the Union soldiers.

Pope thought the battered Confederates would retreat, and promised to follow them. Instead, Jackson

A derailed train is seen near the site of the Second Battle of Bull Run.

received reinforcements and the Confederate Army counterattacked, sweeping the Union forces from the field. The beaten Northern troops plodded back to Washington. Edward Pollard, a Southern editor and historian, wrote, "Now the war was transferred from the gates of Richmond to those of Washington."[9]

After the battle, Brady and several of his photographers came down from Washington, D.C., to photograph the battlefield. They worked for several days. Their photographs illustrated "Jackson's systematic military destruction [and] gave loud testimony to Pope's utter defeat."[10]

7

DEATH AT ANTIETAM

After defeating the Union Army for a second time at Bull Run, General Robert E. Lee decided to invade the North. He marched his troops into Maryland on September 4, 1862. By bringing the war to Northern territory, Lee was hoping to frighten Northerners into accepting an early peace settlement that would be favorable to the South. In addition, a victory on Northern soil might encourage England and France to side with the Confederacy and send ships to break the Union blockade of the Southern coast.

For the second time, Lincoln turned to General George B. McClellan to command the Union Army. With one hundred thousand fresh troops, McClellan marched out of Washington in pursuit of Lee. By a quirk of fate, McClellan obtained a copy of Lee's orders for the Confederate invasion of Maryland. Two Union soldiers found the orders wrapped around cigars in a meadow near Frederick, Maryland. They took the information to Union headquarters. McClellan, however, thought it might be a trap and moved slowly toward Lee's position.

Lee found out that McClellan had a copy of his orders. Realizing the danger, he gathered his army near the town of Sharpsburg, Maryland, along a creek called Antietam.

Battle of Antietam

At dawn on the morning of September 17, the battle began. North of Sharpsburg, Union troops charged into a thirty-acre cornfield. Confederate soldiers, hidden in the woods behind the field, began firing on the Union soldiers. The fighting raged back and forth across the cornfield fifteen times. After four hours, eight thousand men lay dead or wounded.

Battle Names

In the South, battles were generally named after towns. In the North, they were named after landmarks, such as rivers or creeks. Therefore, in the South, this battle was called the Battle of Sharpsburg, and in the North, the Battle of Antietam. Similarly, the Battle of Bull Run was called the Battle of Manassas by Southerners because it was fought near Manassas Junction, Virginia.

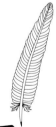

The devastating scene at Dunker Church on the Antietam battlefield in September 1862.

Mathew Brady and several of his photographers followed McClellan's troops into Maryland. They arrived on the outskirts of Sharpsburg shortly after the battle began. From the vantage point of McClellan's headquarters, they had a clear view of almost the entire battlefield. They set up their cameras, and sometime during the morning, took what many historians believe is the only Civil War photograph of actual combat.

Later in the morning, the battle shifted to a rutted country path that divided one farmer's property from

This may be the only photograph of actual combat taken during the Civil War.

another. The pathway was called the Sunken Road. Two Confederate brigades turned it into a rifle pit. As Union soldiers tried to overrun the road, sheets of Confederate bullets hit them. Finally, a group of Union soldiers from New York discovered a spot from which they could fire down on the Confederates in the sunken pathway. The road quickly filled with bodies. In some places, bodies lay three deep. The spot became known as Bloody Lane. When the battle ended, Brady photographed the "ghastly array of dead" soldiers.[1]

Both sides suffered tremendous losses in the battle. The dead and dying covered the battlefield. The Union casualties were 2,108 soldiers killed and another 10,302 wounded or missing. The Confederate losses were 2,700 killed, 9,024 wounded, and about 2,000 missing.[2] McClellan lost a sixth of his army and Lee lost a fourth.

The day after the battle, a truce was called to give both sides time to bury their dead. That evening, under the cover of rain, Lee withdrew his troops from Maryland. McClellan did not follow him.

Brady and his assistants took nearly seventy photographs of the Antietam battlefield. Many of them were displayed in Brady's New York gallery. A *New York Times* reporter commented about the display:

> We see the list [of dead] in the morning paper at breakfast, but dismiss recollection with the coffee. There is a confused mass of names, but they are all strangers; we forget the horrible significance that dwells amid the jumble of type. We recognize the battlefield as a reality, but it stands as a remote one. It is like a funeral next door. It attracts your attention but it does not enlist your sympathy. . . . Mr. Brady has done something to bring home to us the terrible reality and earnestness of the war. If he has not brought bodies and laid them in our door-yards [doorsteps] and along streets, he has done something very like it.[3]

Alexander Gardner Departs

Late in 1862, Alexander Gardner left Brady's employment to go into business for himself. Gardner had worked for Brady for five years. He probably knew

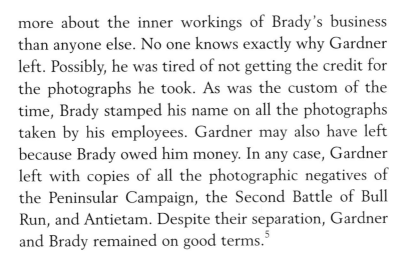

Emancipation Proclamation

On January 1, 1863, President Lincoln signed the proclamation that would free slaves in the Confederate states. Lincoln had spent the morning shaking hands with voters. His right arm was so sore it was nearly paralyzed. When the document was presented to him to sign, he picked up his pen several times and then put it down again. When asked what was wrong, Lincoln replied, "If my name ever goes down into history it will be for this act, and my whole soul is in it. If my hand trembles when I sign the Proclamation, all who examine the document . . . will say, 'He hesitated.'" Then Lincoln picked up his pen again, re-inked it, and with a firm hand slowly signed his name. When he was done, he smiled and said, "That will do."[4]

more about the inner workings of Brady's business than anyone else. No one knows exactly why Gardner left. Possibly, he was tired of not getting the credit for the photographs he took. As was the custom of the time, Brady stamped his name on all the photographs taken by his employees. Gardner may also have left because Brady owed him money. In any case, Gardner left with copies of all the photographic negatives of the Peninsular Campaign, the Second Battle of Bull Run, and Antietam. Despite their separation, Gardner and Brady remained on good terms.[5]

UNDER FIRE AT FREDERICKSBURG

President Lincoln was furious that General McClellan did not go after the Confederate Army after the Battle of Antietam. He replaced McClellan with General Ambrose E. Burnside. A graduate of the United States Military Academy at West Point, Burnside was renowned for inventing a breech-loading rifle and for his side-whiskers. At first, his style of beard was called burnsides, but later became known as sideburns. When the Civil War began, Burnside was a colonel in a Rhode Island volunteer regiment. During the First Battle of Bull Run, he commanded a brigade and was also one of McClellan's corps commanders at Antietam.

Battle of Fredericksburg

Burnside knew he needed to act quickly. He moved his army to the hills on the outskirts of Fredericksburg,

Abraham Lincoln visited General McClellan's headquarters on October 4, 1862. After arriving unannounced, Lincoln questioned McClellan as to why he did not pursue Lee after the Battle of Antietam. Lincoln was so furious that he soon replaced McClellan.

Virginia, where he planned to cross the Rappahannock River, capture Fredericksburg, and then move on to Richmond. Brady and one of his photographers, Timothy O'Sullivan, went with Burnside's troops.

The bridges across the Rappahannock had been destroyed. Burnside had to wait seventeen days for pontoon bridges to arrive to enable his one hundred twenty thousand men to cross the river. This gave the Confederates time to evacuate Fredericksburg and position seventy-eight thousand soldiers in the hills around the town.

When Union engineers began building the pontoon bridges, they were hidden by heavy fog. As they hammered away, sixteen hundred Confederate sharpshooters placed themselves in windows in buildings across the river and patiently waited for the fog to lift. Near the Union engineers, Brady and O'Sullivan set up their camera. When the sun broke through the fog, Brady adjusted the lens on the camera to take a picture. The sunlight reflected on the metal lens. The Confederate sharpshooters must have thought it was the reflection from a cannon barrel. They opened fire. Bullets hit the ground near Brady, upsetting his camera and causing his horses to run away with his darkroom wagon.

Brady ran for cover as O'Sullivan chased the runaway wagon. Eventually, Brady was able to recover his camera undamaged, but the wagon did not fare as well. There were several broken photographic plates and chemical bottles on the floor of the wagon box.

In an attempt to dislodge the sharpshooters, Burnside ordered his artillery to bombard the town. The Union shells hit Fredericksburg at a rate of one hundred rounds per minute. Finally, when it was apparent that the sharpshooters could not be forced out by artillery, several volunteer regiments went across the river to deal with them.

When the sharpshooters retreated to the hills outside of Fredericksburg, Burnside's remaining troops entered the town. Brady and O'Sullivan followed them.

The town had been turned into rubble by the Union artillery. They set up their cameras and photographed the destruction. When the winter light became too weak to continue, they camped in the city streets with the soldiers. No fires were permitted, so they had to eat cold rations.

The next morning, December 13, they were awakened by the sound of artillery. Quickly, they harnessed their horses and drove to the edge of town. Realizing that the weather and battle conditions made it impossible for them to take photographs, they drove back into town. There, they climbed up to the roof of an abandoned house and watched the battle. The Union soldiers advanced twelve times. The Confederates held their ground every time. It was a tremendous slaughter. From their vantage point, the photographers "observed the holocaust through field glasses."[1] The Union Army lost approximately twelve thousand men, and the Confederates lost about five thousand.[2]

The following day, neither side renewed the battle. Burnside wanted to attack again but his staff persuaded him not to. On December 15, a truce was called to permit both sides to bury their dead. The truce allowed Brady and O'Sullivan to photograph the "stricken battlefield."[3] There were so many bodies that they had to be careful not to step on them as they carried their equipment around the field.

That evening, under the cover of fog, Burnside withdrew his troops across the Rappahannock River. It was a shattering defeat for the North.

General Tom Thumb's Wedding

In February 1863, Brady photographed an event in New York City that pushed the Civil War off the front pages of daily newspapers. It was the wedding of two midgets, General Tom Thumb and Lavinia Warren. Twenty-five-year-old Thumb was born of normal parents but only grew to thirty-five inches in height. His bride, Lavinia, was four years younger and one inch shorter. Both were employed by P. T. Barnum.

The wedding took place in Grace Church in New York City. Barnum chose Brady to be the official wedding photographer. Brady was careful to photograph the couple in scale so that their size would be apparent. Cartes de visites of the couple were best-sellers.

On their honeymoon, the Thumbs visited Washington, D.C., and President Lincoln gave a reception for them at the White House. Lincoln's son Tad could not take his eyes off the small couple. He thought Lavinia looked like his mother and remarked, "Isn't it funny that Father is so tall and Mr. and Mrs. Thumb are so little?" President Lincoln overheard his son and commented, "My boy, God likes to do funny things. Here you have the long and short of it."[4]

General Joseph Hooker

Due to Ambrose E. Burnside's poor performance at the Battle of Fredericksburg, President Lincoln replaced him with Major General Joseph Hooker. Brady had previously photographed Hooker and described him as "rather boyish, with red hair, always laughing and in high spirits."[5] For three months, Hooker went about reorganizing and equipping his army. By spring, he had one hundred thirty thousand men at his disposal and President Lincoln ordered him to destroy Lee's army.

Hooker planned to divide his army and attack the Confederates on two fronts. The main part of the Union Army would march up the Rappahannock River, cross it, and then attack Lee's forces from the rear at a place called Chancellorsville, Virginia. As a decoy, another wing of the Union Army would advance on Fredericksburg.

Hooker's maneuvers did not fool Lee, who also divided his forces. On May 2, Lee attacked Hooker's troops outside of Chancellorsville. The Union soldiers were caught completely off guard. They panicked and retreated. In Fredericksburg, the Union troops managed to capture the town, only to retreat back across the Rappahannock River when the Confederates received backups. Once again, Lee had outsmarted one of Lincoln's generals.

Brady and several of his photographers accompanied the Union troops into Fredericksburg. They photographed the battlefield and retreated across the

Rappahannock River with the soldiers. For several weeks after the battle, Brady remained in the area.

One day, Brady was photographing the ruins of Fredericksburg along the banks of the Rappahannock River. After a while, he realized that a group of Confederate soldiers was watching him from the other side of the river. He shouted across the river for them to pose for him.

While he was adjusting his camera to take their picture, the Confederates began to tease Brady about the problems the Union Army was having getting to Richmond. "Before you get to Richmond," they yelled, "you have a 'longstreet' to travel, a big 'hill' to climb, and a 'stonewall' to get over."[6] The soldiers were referring to three Confederate generals—James Longstreet, A. P. Hill, and Stonewall Jackson. Brady laughed along with the Southern soldiers, but when he completed his photograph, he shouted, "We'll get there just the same."[7]

THE TURNING POINT

After the Southern victory at Chancellorsville, Lee desperately needed supplies for his army. Many of his soldiers had no shoes and were marching barefooted. For the second time, Lee invaded the North. This time, he marched his army through Virginia's Shenandoah Valley into Pennsylvania.

On June 28, 1863, Lincoln replaced General Joseph Hooker with General George Meade as the commander of the Army of the Potomac. Previously, the Army of the Potomac had briefly been known as the Army of Virginia. Meade was blunt, bookish, and known for his hot temper. A veteran of the Battles of Fredericksburg and Chancellorsville, he was fondly referred to by his soldiers as a "damned old goggle-eyed snapping turtle."[1]

Battle of Gettysburg

Through intelligence reports, Meade knew that Lee was on the move, but was not sure where he was going. Lee was not certain exactly where Meade's forces were, either. On July 1, 1863, on the outskirts of a small Pennsylvania town called Gettysburg, the two armies collided.

After the initial confrontation, both armies continued to gather their troops around Gettysburg until there were sixty-five thousand Confederates facing eighty-five thousand Union soldiers. On July 2, the Union battle line was shaped like a fishhook. The tip of the hook was at Culp's Hill, the hook curved around Cemetery Hill, and the shank ran along Cemetery Ridge. Two hills called Big Round Top and Little Round Top were also occupied by Union troops and overlooked the battle line. Lee's army was stretched around the outside of the hook.

For two days, the Confederate forces attacked the Union Army's position with little success. The Union battle line held. Then Lee hurled fifteen thousand soldiers at the center of the Union battle line on Cemetery Ridge. It was a massacre. Many Confederates died before they reached the Union battle line. All the men who broke through were either killed or captured.

During three days of fighting, nearly a third of the men engaged in the Battle of Gettysburg—fifty-one thousand men—were either killed, missing, or wounded. The Union Army suffered 23,049 casualties and the Confederate Army 28,063.[2] On July 4, Lee began his slow retreat back to Virginia. He took with him every gun, wagon, and wounded soldier that could be found. His wagon train stretched seventeen miles.

In Washington, D.C., Alexander Gardner and Mathew Brady were now rivals. Gardner had opened a studio at 511 Seventh Street N.W. a few months after leaving Brady's studio. When Gardner learned about the Battle of Gettysburg, he immediately packed up his equipment and headed north. He arrived on July 5, just in time to photograph the rotting corpses on the battlefield and other prominent battle sites. Brady and his assistants arrived a week after Gardner left. Although Brady missed the grim scene after the battle, he benefited from the fact that the landmarks of the battle were well-known and local guides were available to point them out.

Before leaving Gettysburg, Brady went to the home of a local resident, John Burns, a seventy-year-old veteran of the War of 1812. Burns was the only civilian who had fought in the Battle of Gettysburg. Evidently, he became tired of watching the battle, picked up his old musket, and joined the Union troops. He was wounded three times in the battle. Brady drove up to Burns's house in his "what-is-it" wagon and asked Burns if he could take his picture. Burns consented and Brady photographed him sitting on his front porch in an old rocker with his crutches and musket leaning against the wall behind him.

In its August 27 issue, *Harper's Weekly* published engravings of Brady's photographs taken at Gettysburg. In fact, *Harper's* devoted the entire issue to

Brady took this photograph of John Burns, a civilian hero wounded at the Battle of Gettysburg.

documenting the battle. The newspaper credited Brady for making "many of the most reliable war pictures."[3]

Lincoln Portraits

After returning from Gettysburg, Brady's Washington studio took what are probably the most famous photographs of President Abraham Lincoln. On February 9, 1864, Lincoln, accompanied by his ten-year-old son, Tad, visited Brady's studio. Lincoln wore a black broadcloth suit, white shirt, black bow tie, and a large gold watch chain hung through the second buttonhole of his vest. Tad was dressed in a dark suit and also had a gold watch chain hanging through one of his buttonholes.

Eight different photographs were made of Lincoln that day. Then a photograph was taken of Lincoln and Tad together. This was the only time Lincoln was photographed with one of his family members. In order to keep Tad busy during the sitting, Brady posed Lincoln sitting with Tad standing beside him looking at a large picture album with his father. This photograph became popular and many lithograph

This famous Brady photograph of Abraham Lincoln was made into an engraving, which now appears on the Lincoln penny.

Mathew Brady took this famous photograph of President Lincoln with his young son Tad.

copies hung in homes across the country.

General Ulysses S. Grant

A month after being photographed by Brady, Lincoln appointed General Ulysses S. Grant, the hero of the Battle of Vicksburg, as the general in charge of all the Union armies. By capturing Vicksburg, Mississippi, in July 1863, the North gained control of the Mississippi River and cut Confederate supply lines in half. Lincoln had finally found a general who could fight successfully against the Confederates. He

The Lincoln Penny and Five-Dollar Bill

One of the photographs taken by Brady in February 1864 was "the best likeness of my father," according to Lincoln's eldest son, Robert Lincoln.[4] This portrait was later used on the five-dollar bill by the United States Treasury Department. Another side profile of Lincoln taken on the same day was later put on the front of the Lincoln penny.

summoned Grant to Washington, D.C., to announce his appointment and to award him the three stars of a lieutenant general.

When Grant's appointment was announced, *Harper's Weekly* and *Frank Leslie's Illustrated Newspaper* contacted Brady requesting photographs of Grant. Brady could find none that he felt were suitable. So Brady met Grant at the railroad station when Grant arrived in Washington and asked him to come to his studio to pose for a portrait.

The following afternoon, immediately after receiving his commission from President Lincoln, Grant arrived at Brady's studio, along with Edwin M. Stanton, the secretary of war. As Brady was posing Grant, passing clouds dimmed the light in the studio. Brady sent one of his assistants up to the roof to pull off the mat that covered the glass skylights. The operator's foot slipped and crashed through the glass, showering Grant with dozens of pieces of sharp glass. One piece of glass passed close to Grant's face, but he did not flinch.

Secretary Stanton grew pale and pulled Brady aside. He whispered that the incident must be kept secret. "Not a word about this, Brady, not a word! . . . The newspapers will say it was designedly done to injure General Grant! It would be impossible to convince the people that this was not an attempt at assassination!"[5] Brady promised not to say anything about it.

Grant's Plan

Grant realized that the Civil War could not be won in one huge battle nor would it end with the capture of

Ulysses S. Grant was given the rank of lieutenant general when he took charge of the Union armies.

Richmond. He felt a total conquest was necessary to force the Southern people into submission. He was determined to pound the Confederate forces continually until, through attrition (weakening the enemy by attacking continuously), there would be nothing left for them to do but submit.

The Confederate Army was not his only target. He also targeted the Southern people. They had to feel the hardship of war in their homes and daily lives. The war would end only when they could stand no more and begged their leaders to make peace.

Grant planned two major offensives that would be fought at the same time. Under his command, the Army of the Potomac would attempt to defeat Lee's army in Northern Virginia and capture Richmond. In the west, General William Sherman's troops would advance from Chattanooga, Tennessee, into Georgia and capture Atlanta.

In May 1864, Grant's army moved into a desolate area in northern Virginia called the Wilderness and clashed with Lee's forces. Because of the thick forest, cavalry and artillery could not be used effectively. Both armies stumbled blindly through the woods. At times, soldiers became disoriented and accidentally fired on their own comrades. Both sides suffered heavy losses, but no one could claim victory. Brady and some of his photographers accompanied Grant's troops. Photography was impossible in the wilderness. All Brady could do was wait nearby.

Despite heavy losses, Grant was determined to push for a final victory. He repositioned his army and

Union General John Porter and his staff are seen here after the Battle of the Wilderness. At the far right of the photograph, Mathew Brady is leaning against a tree. This is one of many self-portraits Brady made while visiting battlefields.

continued to advance toward Richmond. The two armies clashed at Spotsylvania Court House. Once again, both sides suffered heavy losses, but neither could claim victory.

After the Battle of Spotsylvania, Grant called a council of war at a nearby church. Union soldiers took some of the benches from inside the church and placed them in a semicircle under the trees outside. Grant and his officers sat on the benches and discussed the situation. Brady went inside the church, and from the upper floor, photographed the meeting.

For a second time, Grant regrouped his army and advanced toward Richmond. By June 1, 1864, he had reached Cold Harbor, a small community ten miles east of Richmond. Grant ordered a frontal attack in a final attempt to crush Lee's army. In the first two hours of fighting, seven thousand Northern soldiers were "mowed down."[6] In a period of twenty-nine days, the Army of the Potomac had suffered fifty-five thousand casualties. Many Northerners called Grant a butcher.[7] He realized that many lives would have to be sacrificed to win the war. Still, he would not give up.

Grant changed his strategy. He took his army across the James River and advanced toward Petersburg, Virginia. Petersburg was a vital rail center south of Richmond. Within a short time, Grant realized that he could not capture the city in a single battle. He ordered his men to dig and occupy trenches. The siege of Petersburg began.

In the West, the Union troops under the command of William T. Sherman captured Atlanta, Georgia. Then Sherman marched his troops through Georgia. The men raided houses and farms over a fifty-mile radius, taking anything they could use and destroying the rest. By the middle of December, Sherman occupied Savannah, Georgia, then marched north into South Carolina. When Columbia, the state capital of South Carolina, surrendered, Sherman marched into North Carolina on his way to unite with Grant's army.

In April 1865, Grant seized the Southern railroads that supplied Richmond. This forced the Confederates to evacuate Petersburg and their capital, Richmond.

Lee retreated westward to join forces with the Confederate troops in North Carolina. Grant overtook him and blocked his way. Lee finally realized that to continue fighting would be useless. He sent a message to Grant to set up a meeting to arrange terms for surrender.

Appomattox

On April 9, 1865, Lee surrendered to Grant in the home of Wilmer McLean in the small one-street village of Appomattox Court House. Brady was in Petersburg when word of the surrender reached him. He immediately left for Appomattox but arrived too late. There was nothing left to photograph but the house and the empty room where the peace negotiations had taken place. Union officers had bought or taken everything in the room as souvenirs.

From Appomattox, Brady headed to Richmond. As they abandoned their capital, Confederate soldiers had

Interesting Coincidence
Wilmer McLean also owned a home at the site of the first battle of the Civil War, the Battle of Bull Run. Confederate General P.G.T. Beauregard had used the McLean house as his headquarters during the battle. Ironically, after the battle, McLean had moved his family to Appomattox to get away from the war.

set fire to the city. Brady and his assistant photographed the widespread devastation and gutted buildings.

Robert E. Lee

When Brady learned that Lee had returned to his home in Richmond, he attempted to get permission to photograph him. Brady later recalled, "It was supposed that after his defeat it would be preposterous to ask him to sit, but I thought it would be the time for the historical picture."[8]

Mourning Card

The following "Mourning card" for the Confederate States of America was published in Philadelphia, shortly after the surrender:

Died,

NEAR THE SOUTH-SIDE RAIL ROAD,

On Sunday, April 9th 1865,

The Southern Confederacy,

AGED FOUR YEARS.

CONCEIVED IN SIN, BORN IN *INIQUITY, NURTURED* BY TYRANNY, DIED OF A CHRONIC ATTACK OF PUNCH

ABRAHAM LINCOLN, Attending Physician.

U. S. GRANT, Undertaker.

JEFF DAVIS, Chief Mourner.[9]

Mathew Brady photographed General Robert E. Lee at his home in Richmond, Virginia, a few days after Lee's surrender at Appomattox.

At first, Lee refused, saying, "It is utterly impossible, Mr. Brady. How can I sit for a photograph with the eyes of the world upon me as they are today?"[10]

Brady sought the help of the Confederate General Robert Ould and Lee's wife, Mary. He had known both of them before the war. Lee listened to the pleas of his wife and friend. He agreed to allow Brady to photograph him the following day.

The sitting took place on the back porch of Lee's home. Lee wore the spotless uniform he had worn at Appomattox. First, Brady took a picture of Lee seated alone. Then he photographed Lee along with his son, Custis Lee, and his aid, Colonel Walter Taylor. Finally, Brady photographed Lee standing alone in the doorway. Brady later recalled, "There was little conversation during the sitting, but the General changed his position as often as I wished him to."[11]

10

LATER YEARS

On April 14, less than a week after Lee surrendered, President Lincoln was assassinated while attending a play at Ford's Theatre in Washington, D.C. John Wilkes Booth, an actor and Southern sympathizer, shot Lincoln. A surgeon attending the play examined Lincoln and declared the wound fatal. Soldiers from the audience carried the president from the theater to a boardinghouse across the street. Lincoln died at 7:22 the following morning.

James Bachelder, a publisher, asked everyone present in the room when Lincoln died to visit Brady's studio to be photographed. Bachelder commissioned Alonzo Chappel to do a painting of the deathbed scene. Chappel used Brady's photographs to create a realistic group portrait entitled *The Last Hours of*

Lincoln.[1] In May 1865, *Harper's Weekly* printed wood engravings of President Lincoln's funeral procession in New York City that were drawn from photographs credited to Brady.

Even after the war ended, Brady continued to acquire photographs. He felt that his Civil War collection had to include every possible image. Many photographers made several photographs of the same scene and Brady sought to buy their duplicate images. He also traded negatives with other photographers or borrowed negatives and made copies of them. His collection was so large that he may have purchased bulk quantities of negatives from photographers who did not want to be bothered with storing them after the war.

Grand Review

On May 23 and 24, 1865, two immense victory parades were held in Washington, D.C., to commemorate the end of the Civil War. The first day, May 23, was devoted to the Army of the Potomac, the defending army of the capital under the command of General George Meade. It was a bright sunny day and almost the entire population of Washington, D.C., came out to see the spectacle. Seated in the reviewing stand in front of the White House were President Andrew Johnson, General Ulysses Grant, and other government representatives.

The parade began with General George Meade leading his army "of 80,000 infantrymen marching 12

A Grand Review was held in Washington, D.C., to celebrate the end of the Civil War.

across with impeccable precision." Following the infantrymen were "hundreds of pieces of artillery and a seven-mile line of cavalrymen that alone took an hour to pass."[2] When Meade reached the reviewing stand, he dismounted and joined the other dignitaries to watch the parade. The next day, it was General William T. Sherman's turn. He led the parade, followed by his sixty-five thousand men. It took six hours for them to pass.

Brady set up one of his cameras at the reviewing stand and another on Pennsylvania Avenue near the

Treasury Building. Among Brady's assistants that day was his nephew, Levin Handy. As the columns of soldiers approached Brady's cameras, they attempted to pause long enough for a photograph to be taken.[3]

Bad Times

In 1865, Brady's financial situation was bleak. He had spent his entire savings photographing the war. Now he was living on credit. In order to raise money, on September 7, 1864, he sold half of his Washington gallery to James Gibson, the gallery manager.

The following year, Brady petitioned the New-York Historical Society to purchase his large collection of war photographs. Brady wanted his collection permanently displayed and stored in a fireproof location. His petition received a great deal of support. The Council of the National Academy of Design passed a resolution stating that Brady's collection was "one of great value, as a nucleus of a National Historical Museum, as reliable authority for Art and illustrative of our history."[4]

General Ulysses S. Grant wrote to Brady on February 3, 1866, supporting his decision to have his war photographs placed on permanent exhibition. Grant wrote, "I knew when many of these representations were being taken, have in my possession many of them and I can say that the scenes were not only spirited and correct but also well chosen." In conclusion, Grant noted that Brady's war views "will be valuable to the student and the artist of the present generation" and even more valuable to future generations.[5]

At first, the New-York Historical Society decided to buy Brady's collection, but the sale never took place. Many people were bored with the war. They wanted to put it behind them and go on with their lives. Brady's photographs no longer interested them.

Three years after Brady sold half of his Washington gallery to James Gibson, the gallery went bankrupt. Gibson had evidently collected money owed to the gallery and left for Europe with it, leaving Brady to deal with his creditors alone. The accounting firm of R. G. Dunn & Company concluded in one of Brady's credit reports that "there is no doubt" that Brady "has been badly swindled by the party he sold out to."[6] Brady's Washington gallery at 625 Pennsylvania Avenue N.W. was sold at a public auction. Brady was able to buy back the gallery at the auction for $7,600.

In New York, Brady's main creditor, Anthony & Company continued to harass him for payment. The firm had sold Brady photographic supplies during the war. Finally, it accepted as payment for Brady's debt a complete set of Brady's war photographs. After the settlement, Anthony & Company published many copies of the war photographs, but Brady received no money from them.

In May 1871, R. G. Dun & Company reported that Brady's financial condition continued to be bleak. It stated that Brady was "endeavoring to obtain an appropriation from Congress for the purchase of his views of the War. He has spent a great deal of money now on this object but has not yet been able to accomplish it."[7]

The situation grew worse the following year when William "Boss" Tweed, a close friend of Brady's, was arrested and accused of embezzling millions of dollars from the city of New York. While Tweed held public office, he was able to protect Brady from lawsuits and creditors. Without Tweed's protection, Brady was declared bankrupt by the United States District Court for the Southern District of New York in January 1873. Brady had assets of $12,000, but his debts, to nearly one hundred creditors, totaled $25,000.

Brady returned to Washington and continued to try to get Congress to buy his collection of war photographs. In a letter, Brady wrote,

> I have spent a life-time collecting the works I now offer; I have kept an open gallery at the Capital of the nation for more than a quarter of a century, to assist in obtaining historical portraits and have spent time and money enough, dictated by pride and patriotism, to have made me independently wealthy. In my exertions to save the collection entire, I have impoverished myself and broken up my business and although not commissioned by the Government to do the work I did, still, I was elected by the general consent of the officers of the Government, from the President down, to do the work.[8]

At the time, Brady also transferred ownership of his Washington studio to his wife in an attempt to prevent the studio from being seized to pay his creditors. Later, he mortgaged the studio to his wife's brother, Samuel Handy, and his nephew, Levin Handy.

Two years later, in 1875, Congress appropriated $25,000 to secure title to all of Brady's negatives and

Washington, D.C., as it looked in the years after the Civil War.

prints. Brady used the money to pay off his creditors. He had lost his New York studios, but his gallery in Washington remained open. The studio was heavily mortgaged, but the infusion of cash seemed to energize Brady. Once again, he became the favored photographer in Washington, D.C., for the "powerful and the popular celebrities of the day."[9]

Part of Brady's renewed success lay in the fact that most of his competition had gone west to photograph life on the frontier. Alexander Gardner closed his Washington gallery and went west to become the chief photographer for the Union Pacific Railroad. Many other prominent Civil War photographers, including Timothy O'Sullivan, packed up their cameras and followed Gardner.

Even with renewed interest in his work, times were bad for Brady. Julia, his beloved wife, suffered from a heart ailment and was bedridden. Brady's health was also deteriorating. His poor eyesight had worsened, and he now wore heavy blue lenses in his glasses. He also suffered from painful arthritis. Brady's nephew, Levin Handy, kept the gallery going.

Around this time, Mark Twain, the famous author of *The Adventures of Tom Sawyer* and *Adventures of Huckleberry Finn*, visited Brady's Washington gallery. Brady told a reporter that Twain had toured his gallery and said that, if he were "not so tied up in his own enterprises," he would have liked to publish a book of Brady's photographs.[10] Twain added, they would "make the noblest subscription book of the age."[11] At the time, Twain's publishing company was in the process of preparing Ulysses S. Grant's memoirs for publication.

Due to his financial constraints, in 1881, Brady sold his portraits of Daniel Webster, Henry Clay, and John C. Calhoun to the government. The paintings were made from daguerreotypes Brady had taken of the famous men. For many years, Brady had proudly displayed the portraits in his galleries. The sale of the paintings helped ease Brady's money troubles, but only for a little while. An employee sued Brady for back wages, which led to foreclosure of his Washington studio. Brady was now in his sixties, and even though he had lost his gallery, he continued to work in Washington. At times, he worked under the name Brady & Company with his nephew or in partnership with local photographers.

Sad Old Man

To add to Brady's misery, his wife, Julia, died in 1887. She was buried in the Congressional Cemetery in Washington, D.C. After his wife's death, Brady became a sad, lonely old man who was bad-tempered, quarrelsome, and often drank heavily. For a while, he lived with his nephew, Levin Handy. His eyesight was so poor that he had to read newspapers with the help of a magnifying glass. His only pleasure seemed to be talking with old friends about the past and taking long walks.

One day while crossing the street at Fourteenth Street and New York Avenue, Brady was struck by a horse-drawn streetcar. Bleeding and unconscious, he was rushed to the hospital. When he was discharged, he hobbled about on crutches.

During the summer of 1895, Brady moved to New York City. Brady had been made an honorary member of the 7th Regiment of New York City, a volunteer militia unit. The other members insisted that Brady accept their financial aid. With their help, he rented a room at 126 East Tenth Street in the lower part of the city.

The 7th Regiment also planned to hold a Grand Testimonial Benefit in Brady's honor. The event was to be held on January 20, 1896, at New York City's

In his later years, Mathew Brady was a sad, lonely old man.

Carnegie Hall. General Horace Porter, formerly a member of General Ulysses S. Grant's staff, would serve as the master of ceremonies. After the opening address, Brady would show slides of his photographs of the Civil War. A stereopticon, or magic lantern, as it was commonly called, would project large glass slides made from Brady's negatives on a huge screen. Brady wrote to his nephew, Levin Handy, asking him to supply the slides for the testimonial. Handy agreed to provide 128 slides, but the testimonial never took place.[12] In November 1895, Brady collapsed and was confined to bed with a painful kidney ailment. His health grew steadily worse. On Thursday, January 15, 1896, Brady died at the age of seventy-three.

EPILOGUE

Despite Mathew Brady's many years of fame, his devoted friend William Riley was the only person who came to visit him in the hospital during his last days. After Brady's death, Riley wrote to Brady's nephew, telling him that his uncle "was conscious but for two or three days he was unable to speak on account of the swelling in his throat. I don't think he realized he was dying."[1]

William Riley paid the shipping charges to send Brady's body to Washington, D.C., where he was buried next to his wife, Julia, at the Congressional Cemetery. The final letter Riley wrote to Brady's nephew made it clear just how poor Mathew Brady had become:

I have made a thorough examination of Mr. Brady's effects, and find no papers or other property that it would pay to send you. His wardrobe was only scant, and his coats in number, two . . . an overcoat and frock coat which I gave away. The balance consists of some underwear, a few shirts and socks, etc., not of sufficient [value] to send, and so I thought I would send them to the needy.[2]

Newspapers in New York and Washington printed long obituaries of Brady. The Washington *Evening Star* wrote: "News of his passing will be received with sincere sorrow by hundreds and hundreds who knew this gentle photographer, whose name is today a household word all over the United States. . . ."[3]

When Brady died, Levin Handy was his only heir. After his uncle's death, Handy became a well-known photographer in Washington. He established a long relationship with the Library of Congress. His cameras documented the construction of the library's Jefferson Building, and for many years, he served as the library's only staff member who duplicated photographs.[4]

Mathew Brady's original headstone listed 1895 as the year of his death. On August 1, 1998, a group of Civil War enthusiasts from Warren, Ohio, corrected the error and paid to have a more elaborate headstone placed on Brady's grave.

Legacy

Mathew Brady was a pioneer in the field of photography. Through his knowledge of the new medium and the high standards of excellence he established, he helped bring recognition and respect to the new profession of photography. In addition, he perfected the art of portraiture with a camera to such an extent that he became America's first celebrity photographer.

More importantly, Brady was a historian who understood the role photography could play in documenting history. He is best known for his images of the Civil War. His collection of war scenes represented the first instance of a "comprehensive photo-documentation of a war."[5]

Over the past century, numerous books have been published about the Civil War using Brady's photographs. Ken Burns, the award-winning filmmaker, relied heavily on Brady's photographs in producing his acclaimed television series *The Civil War*. It would have been difficult for Burns to create his series without them.

Today, Brady's photographs can be found at the Library of Congress, the National Archives, and the National Portrait Gallery, a division of the Smithsonian Institution. The images are available to anyone who wishes to see them. Through the images he recorded, Brady and his work live on.

CHRONOLOGY

1823—Born in Warren County, New York (exact date unknown).

1835—Travels to Saratoga Springs, New York, for treatment for the inflammation of his eyes; Meets William Page, an artist.

1839—Arrives in New York City; Meets Samuel F. B. Morse; Learns to make daguerreotypes; Works as a clerk in A. T. Stewart's department store.

1843—Works as an independent manufacturer of jewelry cases at 164 Fulton Street in New York City.

1844—Opens "Daguerrean Miniature Gallery" at 205–207 Broadway and Fulton Street in New York City; Enters American Institute of Photography's annual competition and wins first honors.

1845—Begins collecting photographs of important Americans.

1849—Opens small Daguerrian Gallery in Washington, D.C., at Four-and-a-half Street and Pennsylvania Avenue.

1850—Publishes book entitled *Gallery of Illustrious Americans*.

1851—Marries Juliet "Julia" Handy (exact date not recorded); Travels to Europe with wife and wins medal for photographs exhibited at the Great Industrial Exhibition in London, England; Learns about new wet-plate process for making photographs on paper from a glass negative.

1853—Opens second studio at 359 Broadway over Thompson's Dining Saloon.

1856—Alexander Gardner joins Brady's staff; Begins producing imperial photographs.

1858—Opens National Photographic Art Gallery in Washington, D.C., at 350–353 Pennsylvania Avenue N.W.

1859—Opens third New York studio at 643 Bleecker Street near Broadway.

1860—Opens fourth gallery, the National Portrait Gallery, in New York City at the intersection of Broadway and Tenth Street; Photographs Abraham Lincoln on February 27; Begins producing carte de visite photographs; Photographs Prince of Wales.

1861—Photographs Abraham Lincoln's inauguration on March 4; Battle of Bull Run takes place on July 21.

1862—Peninsular Campaign fought, March–July; Second Battle of Bull Run takes place on August 27–30; Battle of Antietam fought on September 17; Battle of Fredericksburg fought on December 13.

1863—Battle of Gettysburg is fought on July 1–3.

1864—Photographs President Abraham Lincoln and his son Tad on February 9; Photographs General Ulysses S. Grant in March; Sells half of his Washington gallery to James Gibson on September 7.

1865—General Robert E. Lee surrenders at Appomattox Court House on April 9; Photographs General Lee in Richmond a few days after the surrender; President Lincoln is assassinated on April 14; Grand Review victory parade held in Washington, D.C., May 23–24.

1866—Offers to sell his photographic collection to the New-York Historical Society; Financial problems become more severe; Washington gallery sold at auction; Buys gallery and files lawsuit against James Gibson.

1871—Attempts to sell collection of negatives and prints to the United States government.

1873—Files for bankruptcy in New York City.

1875—Receives $25,000 from Congress for his photographic collection.

1881—Sells oil portraits of John C. Calhoun, Henry Clay, and Daniel Webster to the United States government.

1887—Juliet Brady dies.

1895—Struck by horse-drawn streetcar; Moves to New York City.

1896—Dies on January 15 and is buried at Congressional Cemetery in Washington beside his wife.

CHAPTER NOTES

Chapter 1. War

1. Geoffrey C. Ward, *The Civil War: An Illustrated History* (New York: Alfred A. Knopf, 1994), p. 64.

2. William C. Davis, *The First Battle of Manassas: Civil War Series* (Fort Washington, Pa.: Eastern National, 1995), p. 10.

3. Roy Meredith, *Mr. Lincoln's Camera Man*, 2nd ed. (New York: Dover Publications, 1974), p. 11.

4. Ibid., p. 14.

5. Ibid., p. 1.

Chapter 2. Early Years

1. "Still Taking Pictures," *The World*, April 12, 1891, p. 26.

2. Ibid.

3. Ibid.

4. James D. Horan, *Mathew Brady: Historian with a Camera* (New York: Crown Publishers, 1955), p. 6.

5. Mary Panzer, *Mathew Brady and the Image of History* (Washington, D.C.: Smithsonian Institution Press for the National Portrait Gallery, 1997), p. 33.

6. William C. Davis, Brian C. Phonka, and Don Troiani, eds., *Civil War Journal: The Legacies* (Nashville, Tenn.: Rutledge Hill Press, 1999), p. 228.

7. Dorothy Meserve Kunhardt, *Mathew Brady and His World* (Alexandra, Va.: Time-Life Books, 1977), p. 42.

8. Davis, Phonka, and Troiani, p. 226.

9. Roy Meredith, *Mr. Lincoln's Camera Man*, 2nd ed. (New York: Dover Publications, 1974), p. 20.

10. Roy Meredith, *Mathew Brady's Portrait of an Era* (New York: W. W. Norton, & Company, 1982), p. 30.

11. Horan, p. 10.

12. Meredith, *Mr. Lincoln's Camera Man*, p. 20.

13. Ibid.

Chapter 3. Gallery

1. Dorothy Meserve Kunhardt, *Mathew Brady and His World* (Alexandra, Va.: Time-Life Books, 1977), p. 45.

2. William C. Davis, Brian C. Phonka, and Don Troiani, eds., *Civil War Journal: The Legacies* (Nashville, Tenn.: Rutledge Hill Press, 1999), p. 232.

3. James D. Horan, *Mathew Brady: Historian with a Camera* (New York: Crown Publishers, 1955), p. 10.

4. Roy Meredith, *Mathew Brady's Portrait of an Era* (New York: W. W. Norton & Company, 1982), p. 45.

5. Ibid., p. 50.

6. Maud W. Goodwin, *Dolly Madison* (New York: Charles Scribner's Sons, 1896), pp.140–141.

7. Meredith, p. 48.

8. Roy Meredith, *Mr. Lincoln's Camera Man*, 2nd ed. (New York: Dover Publications, 1974), p. 24.

9. Horan, p. 13.

10. Ibid.

11. Meredith, *Mr. Lincoln's Camera Man*, p. 28.

12. Ibid.

13. Dartmouth College, "The Hayne Speech," *Daniel Webster—Dartmouth's Favorite Son*, n.d., <http://www.dartmouth.edu/~dwebster/speeches/hayne-speech.html>, (October 20, 2000).

14. Meredith, *Mathew Brady's Portrait of an Era*, p. 57.

15. Meredith, *Mr. Lincoln's Camera Man*, p. 24.

Chapter 4. Fame

1. James D. Horan, *Mathew Brady: Historian with a Camera* (New York: Crown Publishers, 1955), p. 17.

2. Ibid.

3. Ibid.

4. Ibid., p. 18.

5. Ibid.

6. Ibid.

7. Roy Meredith, *Mathew Brady's Portrait of an Era* (New York: W. W. Norton & Company, 1982), p. 64.

8. William C. Davis, Brian C. Phonka, and Don Troiani, eds., *Civil War Journal: The Legacies* (Nashville, Tenn.: Rutledge Hill Press, 1999), p. 233.

9. Horan, p. 19.

10. Mary Panzer, *Mathew Brady and the Image of History* (Washington, D.C.: Smithsonian Institution Press for the National Portrait Gallery, 1997), p. xvi.

11. Dorothy Meserve Kunhardt, *Mathew Brady and His World* (Alexandra, Va.: Time-Life Books, 1977), p. 48.

12. Ibid., p. 49.

13. Ibid., p. 51.

14. Ibid.

15. Horan, pp. 27–28.

16. Kunhardt, pp. 51–52.

17. Meredith, p. 90.

18. Ibid.

19. Ibid., p. 91.

20. Kunhardt, p. 55.

21. Ibid., p. 154.

Chapter 5. A House Divided

1. Geoffrey C. Ward, *The Civil War: An Illustrated History* (New York: Alfred A. Knopf, 1994), p. 26.

2. Interview with Mary Panzer, *American President's Series, 19th Century Photography of Presidents*, July 16, 1999.

3. Roy Meredith, *Mathew Brady's Portrait of an Era* (New York: W. W. Norton & Co.), p. 99.

4. Ibid., p. 100.

5. Ibid.

6. Philip B. Kunhardt, Jr., Philip B. Kunhardt III, and Peter W. Kunhardt, *Lincoln: An Illustrated Biography* (New York: Alfred A. Knopf, 1992), p. 28.

7. Albert B. Paine, *Thomas Nast: His Period and His Pictures* (New York: Chelsea House, 1980), p. 75.

8. Meredith, p. 110.

9. Ward, p. 62.

Chapter 6. Forward to Richmond

1. Roy Meredith, *Mathew Brady's Portrait of an Era* (New York: W. W. Norton & Co.), p. 106.

2. Ibid., p. 115.

3. Roy Meredith, *Mr. Lincoln's Camera Man*, 2nd ed. (New York: Dover Publications, 1974), p. 117.

4. Richard Wheeler, *Voices of the Civil War* (New York: Meridian, 1990), p. 110.

5. Geoffrey C. Ward, *The Civil War: An Illustrated History* (New York: Alfred A. Knopf, 1994), p. 110.

6. Meredith, *Mathew Brady's Portrait of an Era*, p. 120.

7. G. Allen Foster, *The Eyes and Ears of the Civil War* (New York: Criterion Books, 1963), p. 78.

8. Wheeler, p. 158.

9. Ibid., p. 173.

10. Meredith, *Mr. Lincoln's Camera Man*, p. 123.

Chapter 7. Death at Antietam

1. W. Fletcher Thompson, Jr., *The Image of War* (New York: Thomas Yoseloff Publisher, 1960), p. 57.

2. Mark M. Boatner, *The Civil War Dictionary* (New York: Vintage Books, 1991), p. 21.

3. Cheryl S. Wray, "Photographer Mathew Brady fulfilled his stated objects 'to preserve the faces of historic men'—living and dead," *American Civil War*, vol. 10, September 1997, pp. 20–24.

4. Albert A. Nofi, *A Civil War Treasury* (New York: De Capo Press, Inc., 1955), p. 234.

5. William C. Davis, Brian C. Phonka, and Don Troiani, eds., *Civil War Journal: The Legacies* (Nashville, Tenn.: Rutledge Hill Press, 1999), p. 270.

Chapter 8. Under Fire at Fredericksburg

1. Roy Meredith, *Mr. Lincoln's Camera Man*, 2nd ed. (New York: Dover Publications, 1974), p. 140.

2. Mark M. Boatner, *The Civil War Dictionary* (New York: Vintage Books, 1991), p. 313.

3. Meredith, p. 150.

4. Theodore James, Jr., "Tom Thumb's Giant Wedding," *Smithsonian*, September 1973, p. 61.

5. Meredith, p. 148.

6. Ibid.

7. Ibid.

Chapter 9. The Turning Point

1. Geoffrey Ward, *The Civil War* (New York: Alfred A. Knopf, 1994), p. 215.

2. Mark M. Boatner, *The Civil War Dictionary* (New York: Vintage Books, 1991), p. 339.

3. James D. Horan, *Mathew Brady: Historian with a Camera* (New York: Crown Publishers, 1955), p. 53.

4. Roy Meredith, *Mr. Lincoln's Camera Man*, 2nd ed. (New York: Dover Publications, 1974), p. 160.

5. Ibid., p. 162.

6. The Civil War Society, *Encyclopedia of the Civil War* (Princeton, N.J.: The Philip Lief Group, Inc., 1997), p. 77.

7. Joe H. Kirchberger, *The Civil War and Reconstruction: An Eyewitness History* (New York: Facts on File, 1991), p. 189.

8. Roy Meredith, *Mathew Brady's Portrait of an Era* (New York: W. W. Norton & Co.), p. 144.

9. Kirchberger, p. 258.

10. Horan, p. 59.

11. Meredith, *Mr. Lincoln's Camera Man*, p. 196.

Chapter 10. Later Years

1. Mary Panzer, *Mathew Brady and the Image of History* (Washington, D.C.: Smithsonian Institution Press for the National Portrait Gallery, 1997), p. xx.

2. The Civil War Society, *Encyclopedia of the Civil War* (New York: Random House, 1997), p. 153.

3. Roy Meredith, *Mr. Lincoln's Camera Man*, 2nd ed. (New York: Dover Publications, 1974), p. 204.

4. James D. Horan, *Mathew Brady: Historian with a Camera* (New York: Crown Publishers, 1955), p. 73.

5. Ibid.

6. Panzer, p. xxi.

7. Ibid.

8. Ibid., p. 192.

9. William C. Davis, Brian C. Phonka, and Don Troiani, eds., *Civil War Journal: The Legacies* (Nashville, Tenn.: Rutledge Hill Press, 1999), p. 248.

10. Meredith, p. 239.

11. Horan, p. 86.

12. Ibid., p. 87.

Chapter 11. Epilogue

1. Roy Meredith, *Mr. Lincoln's Camera Man*, 2nd ed. (New York: Dover Publications, 1974), p. 258.

2. Ibid.

3. William C. Davis, Brian C. Phonka, and Don Troiani, eds., *Civil War Journal: The Legacies* (Nashville, Tenn.: Rutledge Hill Press, 1999), p. 87.

4. Mary Panzer, *Mathew Brady and the Image of History* (Washington, D.C.: Smithsonian Institution Press for the National Portrait Gallery, 1997), p. 207, note 52.

5. Library of Congress, Prints & Photographs Online Catalog, *Mathew Brady Biographical Note*, September 22, 1997, <http://rs6.loc.gov/ammem/cwbrady.html>.

GLOSSARY

advance—To move forward.

aerial—Floating or flying in the air.

aroma—A distinctive fragrance.

astronomical—Having to do with astronomy; the science of the sun, moon, planets, stars, and all other celestial bodies.

blockade—Control of who or what goes into or out of a place by an army or navy.

bombard—To attack by firing many guns continuously.

botany—The study of plants and plant life.

commissions—Orders placed to have photographs made.

counterfeit—Something copied and passed as genuine; a forgery.

craze—A short-lived, eager interest in doing something; a fad.

embezzling—The theft of money entrusted to one's care.

exposure—The time needed to make an image on a photographic plate.

field glasses—Small binoculars.

flicker—To shine with a wavering, unsteady light that goes on and off quickly.

fortifications—A wall, fort, ditch, or other defense built to make a place strong.

hardtack—A saltless hard biscuit, bread, or cracker.

haversack—A bag or pouch used by soldiers for carrying food, utensils, and other things when on a march.

lithograph—A print made from a flat, prepared stone or metal plate.

massacre—To kill many people.

negotiations—To confer with another so as to arrive at a settlement of some matter.

offensive—The first attack in a battle.

political machine—A well-organized political group under the control of a strong leader, known as a boss.

reconnaissance—A mission to discover the position and strength of an enemy.

rifle pit—A pit or short trench that shelters riflemen firing at an enemy.

sharpshooter—A person who shoots well, especially with a rifle.

siege—The act of surrounding a fortified place and preventing it from obtaining supplies or receiving communications.

sitting—Posing for a portrait.

souvenir—Token of remembrance; a keepsake.

spectacle—An impressive show or scene.

testimonial—Something that is given or done to show thanks, praise, or admiration.

theatrical—Loud, noticeable, or dramatic.

trademark—Picture, name, word, symbol, or letters owned and used by a manufacturer or merchant to distinguish his or her goods from the goods of others.

tripod—A stand with three legs that holds up a camera.

truce—An agreement to stop fighting for a short period of time.

FURTHER READING

Hakim, Joy. *War, Terrible War*. New York: Oxford University Press, 1994.

Kent, Zachary. *The Civil War: "A House Divided."* Springfield, N.J.: Enslow Publishers, Inc., 1994.

Kunhardt, Dorothy Meserve. *Mathew Brady and His World*. Alexandria, Va.: Time-Life Books, 1977.

Pflueger, Lynda. *Jeb Stuart: Confederate Cavalry General*. Springfield, N.J.: Enslow Publishers, Inc., 1998.

————. *Stonewall Jackson: Confederate General*. Springfield, N.J.: Enslow Publishers, Inc., 1997.

Sullivan, George. *Mathew Brady: His Life and Photographs*. New York: Cobble Hill Books, 1994.

Tibbitts, Alison. *James K. Polk*. Springfield, N.J.: Enslow Publishers, Inc., 1999.

Van Steenwyk, Elizabeth. *Mathew Brady: Civil War Photographer*. New York: Franklin Watts, 1997.

Ward, Geoffrey C. *The Civil War: An Illustrated History*. New York: Alfred A. Knopf, 1994.

INTERNET ADDRESSES

Civil War Photography Center. March 2000. <http://www.civilwarphotography.com/>.

Jones International. "Mathew Brady." *Jones Telecommunications & Mulitmedia Encyclopedia*. n.d. <http://www.digitalcentury.com/encyclo/update/mbrady.html>.

Library of Congress. *Mathew B. Brady Biographical Note*. September 22, 1997. <http://memory.loc.gov/ammem/cwphtml/cwbrady.html>.

Mathew Brady's National Portrait Gallery: A Virtual Tour. n.d. <http://www.npg.si.edu/exh/brady/gallery/gallery.html>.

INDEX